PEMBROKESHIRE FOLK TALES

Brian John

GREENCROFT BOOKS
Newport, Pembrokeshire, SA42 O

Printed in Wales

CONTENTS

	Page
Preface	7
Introduction	8
Glossary of Welsh Terms	11
The Sources of the Stories	12
The Story Locations	15

Section One : Tales of the Saints — 17
- 1.1 St David and the Irish Chieftain — 18
- 1.2 St Justinian and the Giant Axe — 19
- 1.3 St Caradoc in the Rain — 20
- 1.4 The Untimely End of Abbot Pyro — 21
- 1.5 St Brynach's Blarney Stone — 21
- 1.6 The Seven Saints of Mathry — 22

Section Two : Heroic Deeds — 23
- 2.1 Pwll and the Journey to the Otherworld — 24
- 2.2 King Arthur and the Giant Boar — 25
- 2.3 The Heroic Mrs Williams — 26
- 2.4 Anne and the French Prisoner — 27
- 2.5 The Loss of the Lifeboat 'Gem' — 29
- 2.6 The Hero who did not Sleep — 31
- 2.7 The Death of John Poyer — 32

Section Three : Strange Happenings — 33
- 3.1 The Carew Ape — 34
- 3.2 Trouble at Tafarn Newydd — 35
- 3.3 The Nevern Cuckoo — 36
- 3.4 The Last Invasion of Britain — 37
- 3.5 The Lost Child of Pwll and Rhiannon — 39
- 3.6 St Teilo's Skull — 41
- 3.7 Cecil Longshanks and the Toads — 42
- 3.8 Message from India — 42
- 3.9 Harvest Time on Trevalen Downs — 43
- 3.10 Explosion at Druidston — 45
- 3.11 Visit from a Viking — 46
- 3.12 The Fall of Picton Castle — 46
- 3.13 The Mermaid at Aberbach — 47
- 3.14 The Missing Falcon Chicks — 48
- 3.15 Mererid, the Guardian of the Sacred Well — 49
- 3.16 The Wreckers of Marros — 51
- 3.17 Vision at Treffgarne — 52
- 3.18 The Smalls Lighthouse Incident — 53
- 3.19 The Red-Haired Steward of Stackpole — 54
- 3.20 Full Speed in the Fog — 55

3.21 The Flying Farmer of Eglwyswrw 56
3.22 The Colby Moor Rout 57
3.23 Rebecca and her Hosts 59
3.24 A Circumstance at Haverford Castle 60
3.25 Three Brothers of Moylgrove 61
3.26 The Boy in the Bell 62
3.27 The Golden Idol of Trewern 63
3.28 The Sad Loss of the 'Roebuck' 64

Section Four : Fairy Tales 65
4.1 Fairy Folk on Freni Fawr 66
4.2 Gruffydd and the Invisible Islands 67
4.3 The Tempting of Crythor 68
4.4 Elidorus and the Fair Folk 69
4.5 The Old Man of Llech-y-Derwydd 70
4.6 Einon and his Fairy Bride 72
4.7 Peregrin and the Mermaid 74
4.8 Ianto and the Lucky Shilling 76
4.9 The Great Black Snake of Presely 77
4.10 The Mermaid at Porth-y-Rhaw 77
4.11 A Water Horse at Nolton 78
4.12 The Mermaid of Carregwastad 78
4.13 The Old Man in the Cradle 79
4.14 The Little People near Puncheston 80
4.15 The Water Boy at Penyholt Bay 80

Section Five : Witchcraft and Magic 81
5.1 Hannah of Walton West 82
5.2 Sally-Anne of Trefelyn 83
5.3 The Old Black Witch of Cwmslade 84
5.4 The Servant Girl of Gelli-fawr 85
5.5 Abe Biddle and the Hornets 86
5.6 Unpleasantness at Orielton 87
5.7 The Bewitched Cottage 88
5.8 The Launch of HMS 'Lion' 89
5.9 Adam of Roch Castle 90
5.10 Wil Tiriet and the College Principal 91
5.11 Wil Tiriet and the Nolton Coffin 92
5.12 The Bewitching at Walton East 93
5.13 John Jenkin and the Evil Spirits 94
5.14 Abe Biddle and the Missing Jewels 95
5.15 A Troublesome hare at Pontfaen 96
5.16 The Black Calf of Narberth 96

Section Six : Signs, Omens and Portents 97
6.1 The Death Omen at Solva 98
6.2 A Corpse Candle at Tenby 98
6.3 A Corpse Candle in Cwm Gwaun 99
6.4 The Mark of Cain 100
6.5 Phantom Funeral at Penally 100
6.6 Disaster at Landshipping 101

6.7	Phantom Funeral at Cilgwyn	102
6.8	Phantom Funeral at Llanychaer	103
6.9	The Unfaithful Wife of William the Fleming	104

Section Seven: Ghostly Tales — 105

7.1	The Haunting of HMS 'Asp'	106
7.2	David of the Charnel-House	107
7.3	The Bush House Ghosts	108
7.4	Wake Night at Dolrannog	109
7.5	The Vicar and the Headless Lady	110
7.6	Mr Warlow and the Phantom Boat	110
7.7	Goblins on Presely	111
7.8	The Monkton Nun	112
7.9	A Lady in White at Manorbier Castle	113
7.10	The Battle in the Sky	114
7.11	The Phantom Armies of Mynydd Morfil	115
7.12	A Haunting at Castlebythe	117
7.13	The Black Dog of Pant-y-Madog	118
7.14	The Jolly Sailor and the Dog of Baal	119
7.15	Mr Walter and the Phantom Dog	120
7.16	The Cwn Annwn at Laugharne	120
7.17	Broad Haven and the Aliens	121
7.18	Tenby and the Beggar's Curse	122
7.19	Premonition at the Rising Sun	124
7.20	The End of Trefloyne and Scotsborough	125
7.21	Phantom Funeral at Milford	125
7.22	The Ghost of Princess Nest	126
7.23	The Castle Hotel Ghost	127
7.24	Lucy Walter of Roch Castle	128

Section Eight : Folk Heroes, Great and Small — 129

8.1	The Siege of Pembroke Castle	130
8.2	The Pontyglasier Boulder	131
8.3	Tough Times in the Wild West	133
8.4	Tall Tale from Goodwick	135
8.5	The Fools of Strumble Head	135
8.6	The Vision of Rosebush	136
8.7	The Curse at Plas Glyn-y-Mel	138
8.8	How the Wiston Estate was won	139
8.9	The Flying Trousers of Twm Waunbwll	139
8.10	Seithennin and the Drowning of Cantre'r Gwaelod	140
8.11	Black Barty of Little Newcastle	141
8.12	Trouble for an Amorous Bard	143
8.13	Shemi's Wager	144

..... in a flash the great white hound was upon him, placing its huge front paws on his chest and pinning him to the ground. (See p 120)

PREFACE

This is the first comprehensive collection of Pembrokeshire folk tales ever published. For the most part, Pembrokeshire folk tales have been scattered about in books and periodicals dealing with Wales as a whole, and the stories have been difficult to find since most of the important books have long since been out of print. In recent years the most interesting publications to appear have been **Welsh Legends and Fairy Lore** by D Parry-Jones, **Tales of South Wales** by Ken Radford, and a slim booklet entitled **Myths and Legends of Pembrokeshire** by Tony Roberts. But each of these draws heavily on the four classics of Welsh folk-lore, namely **British Goblins** (1880) by Wirt Sikes, **Celtic Folk-Lore** (1901) by Sir John Rhys, **Folk-Lore of Mid and West Wales** (1911) by J Ceredig Davies, and **Folk-Lore and Folk-Stories of Wales** (1909) by Marie Trevelyan. Each of these authors personally collected nineteenth-century stories about Pembrokeshire, and I have attempted to draw them together for this new collection. But the oldest stories, to be found in the writings of Giraldus Cambrensis, in **The Black Book of Carmarthen** and in the collection entitled **The Mabinogion,** may well date from pre-Norman days; some of them go back all the way to the Age of the Saints immediately following the retreat of the Romans from Britain, and at least one story dates back to the Iron Age.

I have made no attempt here to analyse the stories or to look for original sources or connections between them. I leave that task to others better qualified than myself; but to help those who want to research certain stories which might be of interest to them, I hope that my citation of references will be of help.

I should like to thank all those who have helped in the creation of this book, and in particular Malcolm Gordon and Joan Evans at the Haverfordwest Public Library; Robin Gwyndaf of the Welsh Folk Museum; Graham Hadlow for the cover illustration; Sally Rudman for word processing and secretarial help; Rod Crow, Neil Davies and their colleagues at C.I.Thomas & Sons Ltd for their efficiency and expertise in the printing process; and the many Pembrokeshire people who have sent me stories in the post or told them to me in the best storytelling tradition. I am very grateful to Hedd Ladd-Lewis and Luned Tudno Jones who have kindly helped with Welsh translations. Finally I must thank my wife Inger for her constant support and help in listening to the stories, advising on wording, proofreading and a host of other matters.

INTRODUCTION

Every time we listen in our friendly neighbourhood inn to a hilarious story about a local character, or pass on the same story to somebody else, or absorb for future use some particularly fascinating piece of local gossip, we are participating in a tradition which is many thousands of years old. The telling of stories is as natural to us as breathing or eating, and the process is a perfectly respectable part of our culture.

Folk tales tell us a great deal about past events, social and religious customs, lifestyle and economy. They also teach us about ourselves - our likes and dislikes, our morals, our taboos, and our superstitions. Very many tales concentrate on the eccentric, the idiosyncratic, or the unexpected, and so in the telling of them we reinforce the stability of the community in which we live. Without this stability, we as individuals feel insecure, and indeed society itself is under threat.

In Wales, as in Ireland, there is a particularly strong tradition of non-material culture - that is, the culture of words and music, of prose and poetry and song. Story-telling is a part of this culture, and in Wales the art of story-telling was maintained and developed by the bards, those mysterious men who learned the history of their nation, and who taught and entertained their listeners with prodigious feats of memory, with profound insights and with finely-turned phrases. The bardic tradition is kept alive today by the Gorsedd of Bards and by the thousands and thousands of people, young and old, who participate in the annual *eisteddfodau* all over Wales. Mostly the tradition is maintained through the medium of the Welsh language, and many of the oldest stories in Wales (for example, those found in **The Mabinogion**) were told and re-told from generation to generation in Welsh and eventually written down in Welsh. Now those who are not blessed with an understanding of the "language of Heaven" can enjoy these ancient stories in English translation.

Pembrokeshire is particularly lucky in that its rich storehouse of folk tales comes from several cultures. The old county is split into two by that mysterious invisible line called the Landsker. To the north of the line Welsh language and tradition have been maintained for 2,000 years without a break, while to the south the English language gradually replaced Welsh as the language of the common people after the Norman Conquest. Among the settlers who came into the Englishry after the Conquest were Flemings, Anglo-Saxons, Normans, and many thousands of Irish. Each group brought its own story-telling traditions, its own folk memories and its own peculiar way of looking at the world; and each group told its tales, providing extra spice to the rich mix of Welsh tales already circulating in the community. Our multi-racial forefathers were our benefactors, as were those (ranging from Giraldus Cambrensis in the twelfth-century to Richard Fenton in 1811 and J Ceredig Davies in 1911) who had the good sense to write down the best-known tales of their day.

It is not the intention of this little book to **analyse** the folk tales of Pembrokeshire. Its purpose is to entertain, and to that end I have selected 118 of my favourite local stories. I am not particularly concerned about whether they should be classified as myth, legend, folk-tale, anecdote or parable; neither am I too concerned about sources, or authenticity, or accuracy. It is in the nature of folk tales that they change or evolve over time, sometimes improving and sometimes deteriorating with each retelling. Often, as in the ancient tales of **The Mabinogion** there are folk memories perhaps thousands of years old hidden behind the rich tapestries of words; and the sheer complexity of some of these tales can only be explained by the tendency of each teller of each tale, over many generations, to elaborate and exaggerate simply in order to make the tales longer, more enthralling, and richer in local detail. How else can one explain the extraordinary (and irrelevant) detail to be found, for example, in the story of King Arthur and the Monstrous Boar recounted in Tale 2.2, or in the famous stories of Pwyll and his son Pryderi?

The tales in this book come from a wide variety of sources. In my researches I have discovered that the same tale can appear in five or six different versions in the literature, with different names and locations into the bargain. In my re-telling of these tales I have tried to keep as close to the spirit of each tale as possible, sometimes repeating quite closely the wording chosen by another author, sometimes pruning out unnecessary detail, sometimes adding local colour, and sometimes adding probable locations where place-names have been lost over the years. This is all a very subjective process, and so it should be!

But for those who wish to study the folk-tales in greater depth I have listed dates and sources at the end of each tale, and a list of items for further reading is to be found on page 12. I have also added a glossary of Welsh terms which crop up in the tales, and an index (on page 15) to the main locations in which the stories are set. There is no particular geographical bias in the tales; storytelling traditions are clearly equally strong in all parts of Pembrokeshire.

The book is divided into eight sections, with my tales located wherever they seem to sit best. Some tales are difficult to classify, but that is the way with folk tales. We begin with a section entitled **Tales of the Saints** (6 tales), followed by a section on **Heroic Deeds** (7 tales), and a section on **Strange Happenings** (28 tales). Then follows a group of 15 Fairy Tales and a section on **Witchcraft and Magic** (16 tales). There follows a section of nine tales on **Signs, Omens and Portents,** a group of 24 ever-popular **Ghostly Tales,** and a collection of 13 tales called **Folk Heroes, Great and Small** which are difficult to classify elsewhere.

On looking through this book the reader will find a number of parables and deeply moral tales (e.g. 1.1, 3.15 and 4.5) which have no doubt been much used by clerics over the centuries in their exhortations to the faithful. On the other hand there are few if any immoral or ribald tales in this collection. Certainly there are plenty of such tales in circulation, just as there were in Chaucer's day; and no doubt the pilgrims who travelled to St David's told each other much the same sort of stories as those *en route* to Canterbury. But such tales tend to circulate "underground". They are not often written down, and they are therefore ephemeral; it may be also that the heavy constraining hand of nineteenth-century Welsh nonconformity has influenced the published collections of folk tales for Wales as a whole. But while the tales published here may under-represent the role of sex in our storytelling tradition, there are ample compensations. For example, in looking through the tales one finds romance, high adventure, tragedy, treachery, pathos, humour, magic and mystery. One also finds history, for many of the most important episodes in Pembrokeshire history make good stories in themselves, and they have become an invaluable part of our spoken heritage.

Finally, we must always bear it in mind that folk tales are not necessarily **old.** Some of them in this collection are indeed ancient (for example, the story of Mererid (3.15), the tales of the saints and the tales contained in **The Mabinogion**), but it is in the nature of things that many old tales slip into disuse, to be replaced by newer tales which have greater meaning for both tellers and listeners. Thus the story of the Rebecca Riots must have been in wide circulation in the middle part of the last century, just as the story of the Broad Haven alien-visitors was told and re-told *ad infinitum* in Pembrokeshire during the late 1970s. The story of the Presely Goblins (7.7) dates from within the last thirty years, and the story entitled **Trouble at Tafarn Newydd** (3.2) from within the last ten years. Other stories dating from within living memory are, for example, those numbered 2.6, 3.14, 4.14, 7.3, 7.22 and 8.4.

I have also included one tale which, to the best of my knowledge, has never before been written down. It has, however, been told and re-told, and imperfectly remembered, during many convivial evenings in Pembrokeshire over recent years. It is said that alcohol blunts the memory but sharpens the telling of the tale, so it may be that the tale as related here (8.2) bears but little relation to what actually happened. No matter.

What does matter is that all the tales in this book **may** be true. We dare not dismiss them as pure nonsense, and indeed many are well authenticated. The line between truth and fiction is a narrow one; and if we are prepared to suspend our disbelief for just a little while during the reading of these tales we will enjoy them all the more.

And remember, dear reader, that things which lie outside the range of your own experience, or beyond the limits of your own particular set of beliefs, are not necessarily impossible. Are you prepared to swear that aliens have never visited Broad Haven, or that there are no such things as ghosts and fairies, or that phantom funerals are impossible, or that Abe Biddle was an impostor.....?

Brian John
October 1991

GLOSSARY OF WELSH TERMS

Afanc : a water monster, or alternatively a beaver.
Annwn : land of fairies, the underworld, hell.
Bwbach : a sprite, ghost or goblin.
Bwca or Pwca : a familiar spirit, demon or goblin.
Bwgan : an unfriendly goblin or poltergeist.
Canwyll gorff : corpse candle, a light denoting a death or the passage of a funeral.
Ceffyl Dwr : a small but beautiful spectral horse that lives in the sea or in a lake.
Cawr : giant.
Coblyn : a goblin or a spirit knocker in mines and caves.
Consuriwr : a magician or man with special or supernatural powers.
Crachach : gentry.
Crefishgyn : spirit.
Crwth : a stringed musical instrument.
Cŵn Annwn : the hounds of Hell, corpse dogs or sky dogs. They are smaller than the Gwyllgi.
Cyfaredd : charm, fascination, spell.
Cyfarwydd : a skilled teller of stories.
Cyhyraeth : death omen, generally heard but not seen; spectre; phantom funeral.
Cythraul : devil.
Dewin : magician or soothsayer.
Diawl : devil.
Drychiolaeth : apparition or spectre.
Dyn hysbys : a wise man or wizard (literally : a knowing one).
Dynon bach teg : fairies (literally : fair little folk).
Ellyll : elf or goblin.
Gwenhudwy : mermaid or sea divinity.
Gwiber : winged serpent or dragon.
Gwyddon : hag, witch or sorceress.
Gwlad y Tylwyth Teg : Fairyland
Gwrach : hag, witch.
Gŵyll : invisible being, ghost.
Gwyllgi : dog of darkness, spectral hound of huge size, black dog of Baal.
Gŵylnos : vigil or wake.
Hudol : magician or sorcerer.
Noson Lawen : "merry evening" of light entertainment.
Plant Rhys Ddwfn : fairies dwelling on the invisible islands off the Pembrokeshire coast (literally : Children of Rhys the Deep).
Rheibio : to curse or bewitch.
Tân ellyll : will o' the wisp, dancing light over boggy ground.
Tanwedd : death omen in the form of a falling light.
Toili : a phantom funeral.
Tolaeth : death omen such as a tolling bell or the sound of coffin-making.
Tylwyth Teg : fair folk or fairies.
Ychen bannog : oxen of the spirit world, connected with water stories.
Ysbryd drwg : evil spirit or devil.

THE SOURCES OF THE STORIES

Bennett, T. 1982 **Welsh Shipwrecks (Vol 2)**, Laidlaw-Burgess, Haverfordwest, 63 pp.

Bielski, A. 1981 **Tales and Traditions of Old Tenby,** Five Arches Press, Tenby, 108 pp.

Bowen, O. 1971 **Tales from the Mabinogion,** Gollancz, London, 157 pp.

Brinton, P. & Worsley, R. 1987 **Open Secrets,** Gomer, Llandysul, 196pp.

Brooks, J.A. 1987 **Ghosts and Legends of Wales,** Jarrold, Norwich, 144pp.

Coleman, S.J. 1954 **Lore and Legend of Pembrokeshire** (Treasury of Folklore No 26), Mimeo.

Davies, J.C. 1911 **Folk-lore of Mid and West Wales,** Welsh Gazette, Aberystwyth, 341 pp.

Doble, G.H. 1971 **Lives of the Welsh Saints** (ed. D.S. Evans), Cardiff, 248 pp.

Evans Wentz, W.Y. 1911 **The Fairy-Faith of the Celtic Countries,** (Reprint 1981), Humanities Press, Bucks, 524 pp.

Fenton, R. 1811 **A Historical Tour through Pembrokeshire,** London, 388pp.

Giraldus Cambrensis, 1188 **The Journey through Wales** (trans. Lewis Thorpe 1978), Penguin, 333 pp.

Goddard, T. 1983 **Pembrokeshire Shipwrecks,** Hughes, Swansea, 198 pp.

Gwyndaf, R. 1977 **Welsh Folk Museum Tapes** (recordings transcribed in Welsh and English).

Gwyndaf, R. 1989 **Welsh Folk Tales,** Nat. Mus. of Wales, Cardiff, 105 pp.

Howells, R. 1984 **Caldey,** Gomer, Llandysul, 261 pp.

Howells, W. 1831 **Cambrian Superstitions,** Longman, London, 194 pp.

James, J.W. 1967 **Rhigyfarch's Life of St. David,** Univ. of Wales Press, Cardiff, 92 pp.

Jones, F. 1971 'Llanrheithan', **The Pembrokeshire Historian,** No 3, pp 53-80.

Jones, G. 1955 **Welsh Legends and Folk Tales,** O.U.P. London, 230 pp.

Jones, G. and Jones, T. 1976 **The Mabinogion,** Dent, London, 273 pp.

Jones, T.G. 1930 **Welsh Folk-Lore and Folk Custom** (Reprint 1979), Brewer, Cambridge, 255 pp.

Kinross, J. 1974 **Fishguard Fiasco,** Five Arches Press, Tenby 128 pp.

Laws, E. 1888 **The History of Little England Beyond Wales,** Bell, London, 458 pp.

Leach, A.L. 1937 **The History of the Civil War in Pembrokeshire,** Witherby, London, 247 pp.

Lewis, T.P. 1959 **The Story of Wales (Pembrokeshire Edition)** Book One, Llandybie, 181 pp.

Lofmark, C. 1989 **Bards and Heroes,** Llanerch Press, Felinfach, 107 pp

Miles, D. 1984 **Portrait of Pembrokeshire,** Hale, London 223 pp.

Molloy, P. 1983 **And they blessed Rebecca,** Gomer, Llandysul, 352 pp.

Morris, J.P. 1969 **The North Pembroke and Fishguard Railway,** Oakwood, Lingfield, 40 pp.

Paget, P. 1979 **The Welsh Triangle,** Panther, London, 206 pp.

Parry-Jones, D. 1988 **Welsh Legends and Fairy Lore,** Batsford, London, 181 pp.

Price, M.R.C. 1982 **Industrial Saundersfoot,** Gomer, Llandysul, 237 pp.

Pugh, J. 1987 **Welsh Witches and Warlocks,** Gwasg Carreg Gwalch, Llanrwst, 120 pp.

Pugh, R.J. & Holiday, F.W. 1979 **The Dyfed Enigma,** Faber, London, 186 pp.

Radford, K. 1979 **Tales of South Wales,** Skilton & Shaw, London, 180pp.

Rhys, J. 1901 **Celtic Folklore : Welsh and Manx** (2 Vols), Oxford, 717pp.

Rhys, J. et al 1897 **Pembrokeshire Antiquities,** Williams, Solva, 83pp.

Richards, W.L. 1965 **Pembrokeshire under Fire,** Hammond & Co, Haverfordwest, 80 pp.

Roberts, A. 1974 **Myths and Legends of Pembrokeshire,** Abercastle, 32pp.

Roderick, A.J. 1966 **Fortress in the West,** A. & C. Black, London, 152pp.

Scott, V. 1980 **Inferno 1940,** Western Telegraph, Haverfordwest, 76 pp.

Sikes, W. 1880 **British Goblins** (Reprint 1973), E.P. Publishing, Wakefield, 412 pp.

Stuart-Jones, E.H. 1950 **The Last Invasion of Britain,** Univ. of Wales Press, Cardiff, 323 pp.

Styles, S. 1977 **Welsh Walks and Legends, South Wales,** John Jones, Cardiff, 63 pp.

Thomas, W.J. 1952 **The Welsh Fairy Book,** Univ. of Wales Press, Cardiff.

Trevelyan, M. 1909 **Folk-Lore and Folk-Stories of Wales,** Stock, London, 350 pp.

Underwood, P. 1980 **Ghosts of Wales,** Corgi, London, 218 pp.

Vaughan, H.M. 1926 **The South Wales Squires,** Methuen, London, 216 pp.

Warner, P. 1977 **Famous Welsh Battles,** Fontana, London, 160 pp.

Williams, D. 1955 **The Rebecca Riots,** Univ. of Wales Press, Cardiff, 377 pp.

Williams, H. 1975 **Battles in Wales,** John Jones, Cardiff, 56 pp.

Williams, J. 1971 **Give Me Yesterday,** Gwasg Gomer, Llandysul, 154pp.

Webb, H. 1984 **Tales from Wales,** Dragon, London, 95 pp.

Worsley, R. 1988 **The Pembrokeshire Explorer,** Coastal Cottages, Abercastle, 127 pp.

THE STORY LOCATIONS

Aberbach 3.13
Abercuch 2.1
Amroth 3.16, 4.3

Bishops and Clerks 2.3
Bitches 1.2, 2.5
Boncath 4.8
Broad Haven 7.17
Bush House 7.3

Caerfarchell 5.10
Caersalem 5.4, 6.7, 7.4
Caldey Island 1.4
Canaston Bridge 3.22
Cantre'r Gwaelod 3.15, 8.10
Cardigan 3.25, 8.9
Cardigan Bay 3.13, 3.25, 4.7, 4.10
Carn Alw 4.5
Carew 3.1, 7.22
Carningli 1.5, 7.4
Carregwastad 3.4, 4.12
Castle Pill 7.6
Castlebythe 5.3, 7.10, 7.11, 7.12
Cemais Head 4.7
Cenarth 4.13
Cilciffeth 7.10, 7.11
Cilgwyn 6.7, 7.4
Clegyr Boia 1.1
Crymych 4.1, 8.9
Colby Moor 3.22
Cold Blow 5.16
Cot Moor 7.15
Cwm 7.14
Cwm Cerwyn 2.2
Cwmslade 5.3
Cwm Gwaun 5.4, 6.3, 6.8, 7.4, 7.7, 7.10, 7.11, 7.12, 7.14

Daugleddau 6.6, 7.1
Devil's Nags 7.15
Dolrannog 7.4
Druidston 3.10

Efailwen 3.23
Eglwyswrw 3.21, 5.25

Fachelich 5.11
Fishguard 3.4, 5.5, 5.14, 7.14, 8.7

Foelfeddau 7.7
Freni Fach/Fawr 4.1

Gelli-fawr 5.4
Glandwr 8.9
Glyn Cuch 2.1
Glyn Rhoson 1.1
Glyn-y-Mel 8.7
Goodwick 3.4, 8.4, 8.13
Gwaun Valley: see Cwm Gwaun

Haverfordwest 2.4, 3.22, 3.24, 5.10, 5.12, 8.3, 8.12
Herbrandston 3.10, 6.4

Lamphey 8.1
Landshipping 6.6
Laugharne 7.13, 7.16
Lawrenny 7.1
Linney Head 4.15
Little Haven 5.1, 7.17, 7.23
Little Newcastle 8.11
Llanddewi Brefi 1.5
Llandeilo Farm 3.6
Llanrheithan 8.3
Llanwnda 4.12
Llanwnwr 8.5
Llanychaer 6.3, 6.8
Llanychllwydog 6.8
Llawhaden 3.22
Llechryd 3.8
Llech-y-Derwydd 4.5
Lundy Island 3.20

Maenclochog 4.9, 8.5
Manorbier 7.9
Manordeifi 3.8
Marros 3.16
Mathry 1.6, 5.2
Merlin's Bridge 1.3
Middle Mill 5.10
Milford Haven 2.4, 7.6, 7.21, 8.1
Monkton 3.11, 7.8
Moylgrove 3.25
Mynachlogddu 3.23
Mynydd Castlebythe 5.3
Mynydd Morfil 7.10, 7.11
Mynydd Presely, see Presely Hills

Narberth 2.1, 3.5, 5.16
Nevern 1.5, 3.3, 3.7
Newgale 1.3
New Inn 3.2
Newport 3.27, 6.7, 7.19
Neyland 3.28
Nolton 4.11, 5.11

Orielton 5.6

Panty-y-Madog 7.13
Pembroke 2.4, 7.3, 8.1
Pembroke Dock 2.6, 5.8, 7.1
Penally 6.5
Penbiri 4.10
Pencaer 3.4, 4.12, 8.6
Pendine 3.16, 4.3
Pentre Ifan 3.27
Penyfeidr 3.17
Penyholt Bay 4.15
Picton 3.12
Pill 7.2, 7.21
Pontfaen 5.15, 6.3, 7.7, 7.10
Pontyglasier 8.2
Poppit Sands 4.7
Porth-y-Rhaw 4.10
Porthclais 2.2, 2.5
Porthlysgi 1.1
Porthselau 2.3
Porthstinian 1.2
Presely Hills 2.2, 3.2, 4.1, 4.5 4.6, 4.14, 5.3, 7.10, 7.11, 7.12, 8.2, 8.6, 8.11
Puncheston 4.14, 5.3, 8.11

Ramsey Island 1.2, 2.5
Ramsey Sound 1.2, 2.3, 2.5
Ripperston Farm 7.17
Roch 5.9, 7.24
Rosebush 3.2, 8.5

St Bride's Bay 1.3, 3.10, 4.11
St Clears 5.7
St David's 1.1, 3.26, 4.2, 4.4
St Dogmaels 3.14, 4.7
St Govans 3.9
St Justinians 1.2
Sampson Cross 7.5
Scotsborough 7.20
Slebech 3.22
Smalls Lighthouse 3.18

Solva 3.18, 6.1
South Hook Fort 6.4
Spittal 1.6
Stack Rocks 7.16
Stackpole 3.19, 7.5
Strumble Head 8.5

Tafarn Newydd 3.2
Tenby 2.7, 6.2, 7.18
Trefelyn 5.2
Treffgarne 1.6, 3.17
Trefloyne 7.20
Trehowel Farm 3.4
Treleddyn 2.3, 3.4
Trellyffaint Farm 3.7
Treseissyllt Farm 3.13
Trevalen Downs 3.9
Trewern 3.27
Ty-rhyg 5.3

Walton East 5.12
Walton West 5.1
Werndew 5.5, 5.14
Whitland 5.7
Wiston 8.8

PEMBROKESHIRE FOLK TALES

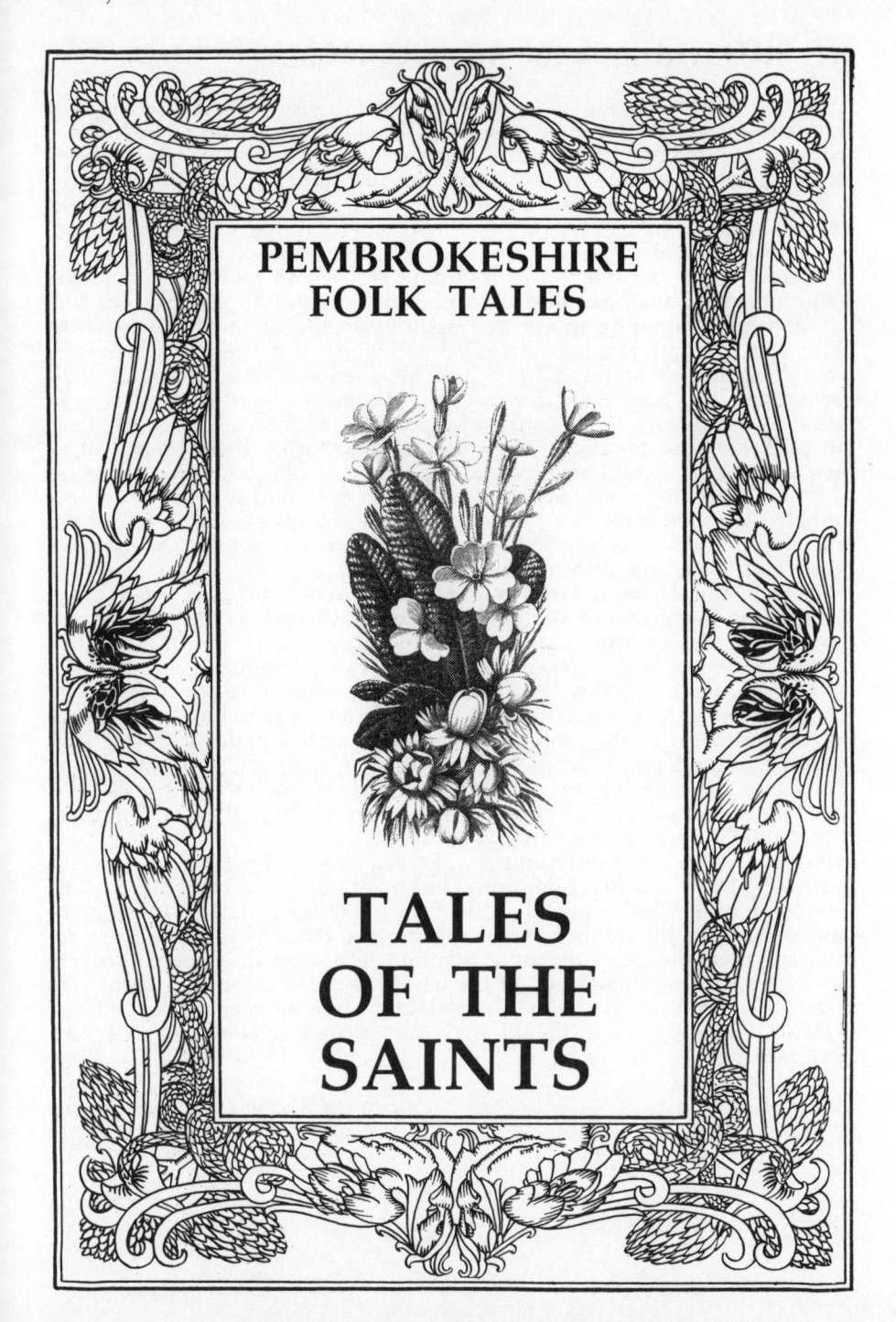

TALES OF THE SAINTS

1.1 St David and the Irish Chieftain

At the end of his missionary travels around the year 560 AD, Dewi (who was later to become Dewi Sant or Saint David) returned to Glyn Rhoson with his faithful friends including Aidan, Teilo and Ismael, having been told by an angel that he must found a monastery in the land of his birth.

To celebrate their arrival the friends lit a fire. The smoke curled lazily towards the rocky hillock of Clegyr Boia, where an old Iron Age hill fort had been occupied by an Irish chieftain and his family. Boia (for that was his name) had terrorised the surrounding lands, and he was furious that some intruder was apparently preparing to settle not a mile from his fort without even bothering to ask permission. On the insistence of his wife (who was a very forceful woman) he gathered up his fighting men and went charging off to teach Dewi and his friends a lesson. But as they approached the holy men they were overcome by a strange fever and retreated in disarray. They returned home to face the wrath of Mrs Boia; but as if that was not bad enough they found that in their absence all of their cattle and sheep had mysteriously dropped dead. Realising that he was dealing with forces beyond his control, Boia returned to Dewi and humbly requested mercy for himself, his men and his beasts. In return for obtaining possession of the site earmarked for his monastery, David made peace with Boia and restored his animals to life.

So Boia and Dewi became friends. But Boia's wife was even more incensed at the presence of the holy men, and resorted to all sorts of devices in order to drive them away. One of her ploys was to send her female slaves to bathe naked in front of Dewi's monks, and to play suggestive games and "use lewd words". The monks were sorely tempted, and implored Dewi to leave the area. But their leader remained strong, and he restored order in the monastic community after a night of fasting and prayer. By now Boia's wife was on the verge of madness. In a last gesture of defiance she carried her step-daughter Dunawd down to the bank of the River Alun and sacrificed her to the pagan gods. Then she fled from the scene, totally mad, never to be seen again.

Boia did not last much longer. He decided to revenge himself by destroying Dewi and his community, but before he could bring his plan to fruition another Irish chieftain called Lysgi (after whom Porthlysgi is named) invaded his camp without warning and cut off his head. Then, to complete this episode of devine retribution, fire came down from heaven during a great thunderstorm and the whole of Boia's camp was destroyed in a blazing inferno. Over 1400 years later, when archaeologists came to excavate at Clegyr Boia, they found the charred remains of huts and storehouses.....

Date : c 560 AD   Sources : Worsley p.37, Fenton p.67

1.2 St Justinian and the Giant Axe

It is said that Justinian was a strict ascetic who arrived on the coast of the St David's peninsula in a vessel of woven osiers and hides tanned in oak bark and rubbed with the grease from sheep's wool. We do not know precisely where he landed, but it may have been on Ramsey, which was at that time connected to the mainland by an isthmus or narrow causeway of rock.

Like Dewi and his followers, Justinian lived a life of simplicity, hard physical toil and devotion. He shunned personal possessions, seldom talked, and lived for the most part upon bread, water and wild fruits. He became the friend and confessor of Dewi, but tired of the communal monastic life and determined to lead a more spiritual life as a hermit. So he retreated to Ramsey in order to find peace and to spend his time in prayer and contemplation. But as his fame spread, more and more disciples came to visit him and before long there was a monastic community on Ramsey as well. Justinian still longed to be far from the madding crowd, and prayed for deliverance. In answer to his prayer a heavenly hand appeared, wielding a mighty axe. It began to chop away the Ramsey causeway at its eastern end, with great success at first; but as the giant blows fell towards the western end of the causeway the axe became more and more blunt, so that the task was never completed. The result is the set of fearsome rocks called The Bitches and Whelps, projecting through the waters of Ramsey Sound and causing the tide race to roar and boil through the jagged pinnacles. The closest cut to the island is still known as The Axe.

.... pilgrims and disciples continued to plague him, now travelling to Ramsey by boat instead of on foot.

Poor Justinian still failed to find the solitude he desired, for pilgrims and disciples continued to plague him, now travelling to Ramsey by boat instead of on foot. He became more irritable, more eccentric and more ascetic, constantly admonishing his monks for their lax ways and urging them to greater and greater self-disciplne and self-denial. At last they could stand it no longer, and they murdered him by chopping off his head. At once a holy spring of crystal clear water began to flow from the spot where his head fell to earth. But our friend Justinian was nothing if not resilient. Undeterred, he picked up his head, walked across the waters of the sound to Porthstinian, and there laid himself down. In celebration of the miracle a chapel was built on the spot where he died, near another holy well and not far from the top of the steps that now lead down to the lifeboat station. The murderous monks were struck down with leprosy and were banished to the barren rock of Ynys y Gwahan to work out their penance.

After all this Ramsey became even more famous as a holy island. Two chapels were built there, and there is an ancient burial ground near the site of the farmhouse. It is said that 2,000 saints are buried beneath the island's lush green turf.....

Date : c 580 AD ?   *Sources : Fenton p.70, Miles p.92*

1.3 St Caradoc in the Rain

Caradoc was one of the later Celtic saints associated with Pembrokeshire. After many years as a hermit the time came for him to depart this life, and he ended his days ("happily enough", according to Giraldus) in 1124. There was some dispute about where he should be buried, but at last it was decided, according to his dying wish, to take his body from his hermit's cell near Merlin's Bridge to St David's Cathedral. As his body was being carried by his disciples across Newgale Sands the clouds opened and there was a tremendous rainstorm, causing the whole countryside to run with water. Those who were in charge of the holy cortege ran for shelter, leaving the body on the beach. When the rain stopped they emerged and returned to the body, to find that the bier and its silken pall were completely dry, and not even dampened by the rain. Celebrating this miraculous occurrence, Caradoc's disciples carried the body on to St David's, where it was buried with due solemnity. Later on, a small chapel made with boulders from the beach was built near the spot where the miracle occurred.

Date : 1124   *Sources : Fenton p.81, Giraldus p.145*

1.4 The Untimely End of Abbot Pyro

Caldey Island is named, in Welsh, Ynys Pyr or the Isle of Pyro. Pyro - or St Pyro as he is sometimes called - was the first abbot of the Caldey monks, probably having been appointed by St Illtyd to look after the little community whose daub and wattle cells surrounded the first Caldey chapel.

We do not know much about Pyro except that his saintliness was open to question. According to the old records, he wandered about the settlement one dark night "in an unseemly drunken bout", having consumed too much of the local wine. He came into the precincts of the monastery, presumably feeling extremely happy and singing at the top of his voice, whereupon he fell into a deep well. He shouted for all he was worth, and indeed succeeded in rousing the brothers from their slumbers (if they were not awake already), but by the time they discovered where he was he was half drowned. They managed to haul him out, but he was almost dead, "and so he died that night".

Later on, there were moves to sanctify Pyro, but one medieval scholar who read his story "in utter loathing" ascertained that his special mark of sanctity was simply "that he fell into a well while drunken with wine, and thus died". Perhaps we should remember him as the patron saint of drunkards.....

Date : c 450 AD ?   *Sources : Doble p.57, Howells p.21*

1.5 St Brynach's Blarney Stone

St Brynach was an Irish monk who was a contemporary and friend of Dewi Sant. Legend has it that he lived part of his life at Nevern, and that he spent long periods communing with the angels from a simple cell at the summit of Carningli. Like St Francis of Assisi, he was renowned for his understanding of birds and other animals. He was also apparently well blessed with the art of the blarney.

Dewi often stayed with his friend on his journeys between his monastery at St David's and his other monastic community at Llanddewi Brefi. One day Brynach was amazed to see his old friend arriving with an elaborately carved Celtic cross on his back. The stone was magnificent, 13 feet high and two feet wide, with a superb pattern of endless interlacing cords cut into its surface, and surmounted by a beautiful Celtic wheel cross. Impressed with his friend's superhuman strength (for the cross was indeed a mighty burden), Brynach asked Dewi what he was going to do with it. Dewi replied that he was taking it to Llanddewi Brefi, where it would be set up as a memorial to himself. Brynach liked the look of the stone, and in true Irish style he soon convinced Dewi that it was really rather arrogant to carry around a monument to oneself. Besides, he would probably do himself an injury in carrying such a weight all that way. Dewi had to agree that for the good of his own soul and the greater glory of God he should leave the stone at Nevern. And there it stayed, eventually to become known as "St Brynach's Cross".....

Date : c 580 AD   *Source : Western Telegraph 30.8.89*

1.6 The Seven Saints of Mathry

Once upon a time, a long time ago, there was a poor man called Cynwayw, who lived with his wife in a hovel not far from Spittal. It happened that she was very heavy with child, and in due course she gave birth to septuplets, all seven of them being boys. Although the babies were all healthy, the father was distraught, for it was midwinter and he knew that his poor wife could not feed all of them, nor could he possibly provide for them as they grew up. He knew that they would probably die of starvation or disease. So with a heavy heart he took the babies down to the River Cleddau near Treffgarne and determined to drown them.

Just as Cynwayw was about to perform his heinous act, the good St Teilo came by and commanded him to stand back from the river bank. He baptised the babies there and then, and realising the father's terrible dilemma, took them with him. He brought them up as best he could, and then sent them to be taught by St Dyfrig in the ways of the church. When they had reached adulthood he sent them to Mathry, where they were renowned for their good works and became known as the "seven saints of Mathry". And there, when they died, they were interred in stone coffins in the circular churchyard. Later on, a stone church was built on the site, and it was dedicated to the Seven Saints.

Date : c 550 AD ?
Source : Miles p.75

Just as Cynwayw was about to perform his heinous act, the good St Teilo came by ...

PEMBROKESHIRE FOLK TALES

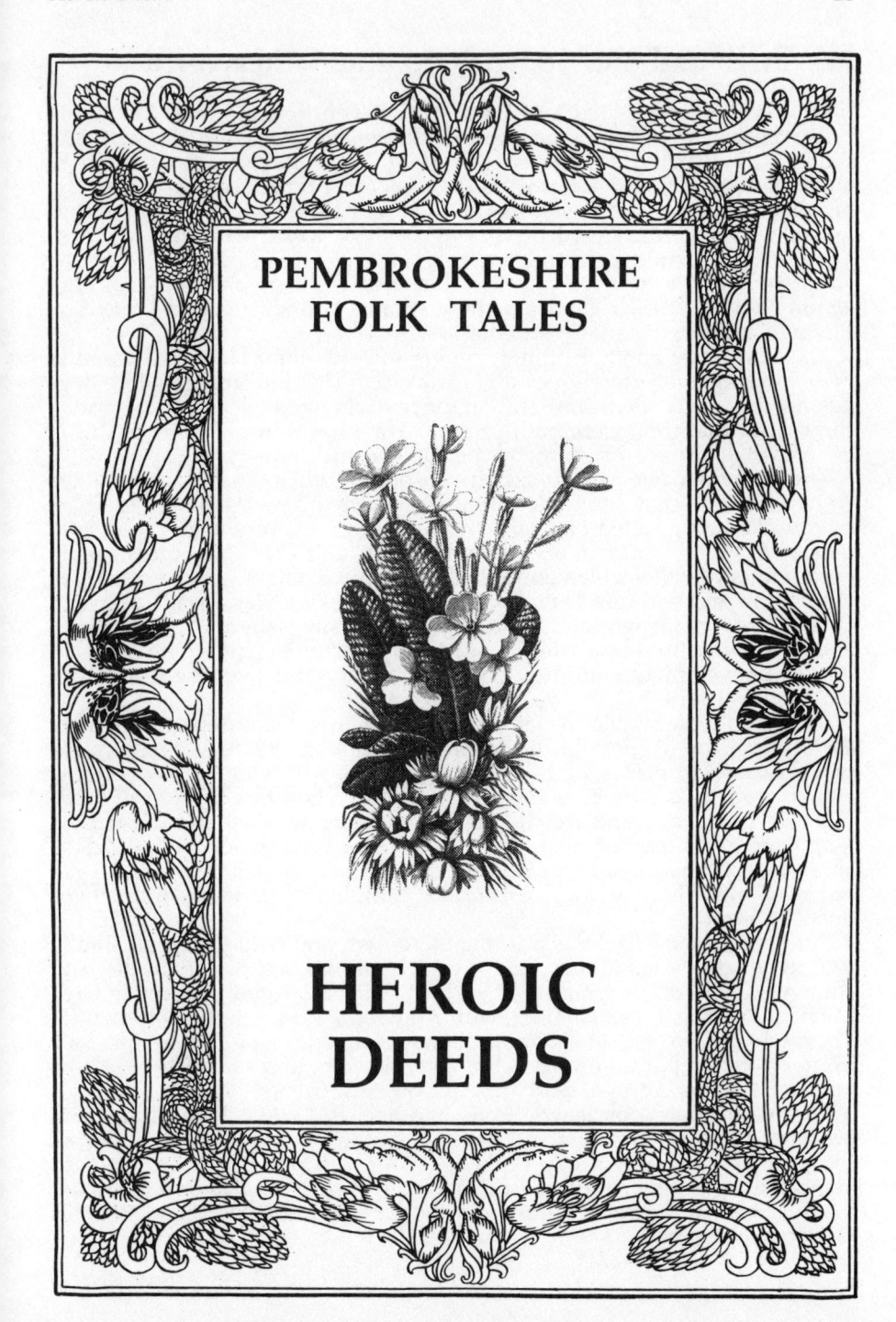

HEROIC DEEDS

2.1 Pwll and the Journey to the Otherworld

Pwll was Prince of Dyfed and Lord of its Seven Regions, well loved and respected by his people. One day he left his chief palace at Narberth and rode to Glyn Cuch for a day's stag-hunting. The valley was deep and dark and well-wooded, and soon his hounds picked up the scent of a stag. He and his companions followed the hounds, but then Pwll lost them and as he rode on alone he heard the baying of dogs which were not his own. Soon he came across a clearing where a fine stag was at bay, circled by the strangest hounds he ever saw; for they had red ears and red eyes, but shining white bodies. Pwll drove these strange hounds away and called on his own hounds to attack the stag.

Then Pwll saw another hunter coming towards him. He was dressed in grey and rode on a grey horse, and it was clear that the strange white dogs belonged to him. Pwll and the stranger exchanged pleasantries, and it turned out that they were both princes. The hunter in grey turned out to be Arawn, a Prince of Annwn, the Otherworld.

The two men felt a great affinity to one another, and as they talked Arawn made a suggestion. He said that in Annwn he was greatly troubled by a wicked king called Havgan. "If you will go to Annwn in my stead," he said to Pwll, "you will be able to rid me of this tyrant. By means of an enchantment I will enable you to go there in my likeness, while I remain in your realm and will rule here in your likeness." Pwll was always prepared to take on a challenge, and he agreed to this suggestion. "But beware," added Arawn. "In a year from tonight you will fight a battle with Havgan. You will have him at your mercy, but you must not deliver the final stroke that will kill him."

So Arawn took Pwll to his kingdom, and the two men exchanged places, each one in the likeness of the other. Pwll thought his new kingdom the most beautiful of places, and he lived there for a year, wanting for nothing, enjoying all life's pleasures and ruling wisely. Then the day of the battle with Havgan came, and watched by all the warriors Pwll and the wicked king joined in mortal combat. Pwll was a fearsome warrior, and struck so shrewdly with his sword that Havgan's shield was shattered. Then Havgan implored him "For the love of Heaven, complete your work. I see that I must be slain".

But Pwll remembered the warning of Arawn, and held back, refusing to deal the death blow. And in this way Havgan was taken away to die, and Annwn was rid of his tyranny. Then Pwll rode back to the clearing in Glyn Cuch and met again, as planned, with Arawn the Prince of the Otherworld. They rejoiced to see one another, and each was restored to his own likeness. Pwll reported on his battle with Havgan, and said "There is now but one lord in Annwn, and that is you, my friend".

The two friends took leave of one another, and when Pwll returned to his palace at Narberth he asked his nobles how his rule had been during the past year. "Lord," they replied, "Your wisdom has never been so great, nor your generosity so free, nor your justice so true and magnanimous." So Pwll swore to continue in the good ways of his friend, and his kingdom prospered.

Date : 800-900 AD ?   Sources : Bowen p.13, Roberts p.2, Webb, p.13

2.2 King Arthur and the Giant Boar

One of the ancient stories related in **The Mabinogion** concerns a heroic running battle between King Arthur and his knights and a Monstrous Boar called Twrch Trwyth. The unwitting cause of all the trouble was a young prince called Kilhwch, who was madly in love with a young lady called Olwen, whom he had never met. The girl's father was a wicked giant called Yspaddaden Penkawr, who set all suitors an assortment of seemingly impossible tasks in order to win her hand in marriage. Anyway, to cut a very long story short, King Arthur had agreed to help this young prince in the performance of a number of terrible tasks, which they achieved by means of guile and not a little magic. At last only one task remained - that of stealing a comb, razor and scissors from between the ears of the great boar, a bad-tempered beast who had once been a wicked Irish King.

When King Arthur travelled to Ireland to ask politely for the comb, razor and scissors Twrch Trwyth refused to speak to him, let alone make him a present of the desired objects, and instead he swam across to Wales, accompanied by seven young ferocious boars, to ravage Arthur's territory. The boars landed at Porthclais near St David's and laid waste the districts around Milford Haven before Arthur and his knights caught up with them and pursued them to the Presely Hills. They fought one battle in the Nevern Valley and then another great and bloody battle in Cwm Cerwyn, the deep depression beneath the summit of Presely. Here four of Arthur's knights were killed. Turning at bay a second time the beast slew four more knights and was wounded himself, while several of the young boars were also killed. The chase continued to Llandissilio, then into Cardiganshire, then all over South Wales, with many local people falling victim to the boars and with four more knights slain.

At last only Twrch was left. He was forced to swim out into the Severn estuary, where Arthur managed to grab the razor and scissors from between his ears. The comb was not obtained until the chase reached Cornwall, and then the great boar leaped into the sea and was never seen again.

Armed with the razor, scissors and comb, Arthur cut Kilhwch's hair and gave him a shave. Then he helped him to kill the savage giant called Yspaddaden Pendawr (who was, you may recall, Olwen's dad), thereby enabling the handsome prince and the beautiful girl to get married and live happily ever after.

Date : c 1050 ?   Sources : G. Jones p.105, Jones & Jones p.132, Roberts p.5

2.3 The Heroic Mrs Williams

The farm called Treleddyn, above Porthselau beach, has figured prominently in the social history of the St David's Peninsula. It was Mr Williams of Treleddyn who first recognized the French vessels carrying the invasion force of 1797, and who rode all the way to Fishguard, keeping the vessels in view, to raise the alarm. However, a few years earlier an incident occurred which deserves a special place in the annals of heroism at sea.

Mrs Margaret Williams was the farmer's second wife, having married him in 1791. The couple kept a small boat complete with sails and oars on the beach at Porthselau. In 1793 they were semi-retired, so they spent a great deal of their time gazing through their telescope at ships passing back and forth along the coast. Sometimes there were in excess of a hundred vessels passing through Ramsey Sound in a single day. One day, at the height of a terrible storm, Mrs Williams sighted through the telescope a group of shipwrecked mariners hanging on to one of the smaller rocks of the Bishops and Clerks, lashed by fierce winds, breaking waves and driving spray. Realising that they were in mortal danger of being swept away, and being in better health than her husband, she immediately launched the small boat and rowed out across Ramsey Sound to save them. She must have rowed at least five miles in order to reach the rock to the east of Carreg Rhoson, where she found seven Swedish sailors in fear of their lives. They had virtually given up hope of rescue, having had no food or shelter to sustain them. They had begun to carve a message concerning their "melancholy story" onto the rock with a knife when they spotted their rescuer approaching. It transpired that their vessel carrying pig iron had been wrecked, and that one of their number had been lost as the ship went down. With great difficulty Mrs Williams got the men on board her frail craft and rowed them back through mountainous seas to Porthselau and safety.

Back at Treleddyn the brave lady provided the shipwrecked sailors with dry clothing, food, warmth and shelter until they had recovered from their ordeal. While everyone knows the heroic tale of Grace Darling (who helped her father in a brave sea rescue in 1838) Mrs Williams' heroism is not widely known even locally; but the Swedish sailors did not forget their rescue or their rescuer, and near the small village of Öregrund in Sweden there is said to be a plaque which commemorates the event.

Date : 1793 ?   *Sources : Bennett p.6, Goddard p.70, Worsley p.57*

2.4 Anne and the French Prisoner

Following the abortive French Invasion of February 1797, a mottley collection of prisoners was held for a while in Haverfordwest. Most of them were locked up in Haverfordwest Gaol, but others were kept in St Mary's Church. Among these were the young son of the Marquis de Saint-Amans and a grenadier sergeant called Roux. A number of local girls were hired to bring food to the prisoners, including Anne Beach, a wealthy young lady who was sister-in-law to the Vicar of St Mary's, and her friend Eleanor Martin. As their visits to the prisoners continued she and the young French nobleman fell in love, as did Eleanor and Sergeant Roux. Soon the majority of prisoners who were fit enough to travel were transported to Portsmouth, and those who remained were moved to Haverfordwest gaol. For some reason - possibly because they had been injured during the fighting - the young nobleman and his friend were among a group of about 190 left behind in the county town. The girls contrived to meet their heroes under most difficult circumstances, and agreed to correspond with them when they were sent on to other prisons. Eventually Anne promised that she would marry her young nobleman when he was released.

In March the prisoners were ferried across the Haven to the notorious Golden Prison, a little way outside the town of Pembroke, to await eventual deportation to the prisoner-of-war hulks in Portsmouth Harbour. The young ladies followed them and convinced the jailers to allow them to carry daily food supplies into the prison. This they did, coming and going regularly with baskets of food and pails of water. Throughout the Spring and early Summer the love affairs flourished; but the young couples could spend no time alone and lived constantly under the threat of the impending arrival of the prison ships. But the ships did not come.

Most of them were locked up in Haverfordwest Gaol......

As the days stretched into weeks and then months, the resourceful Anne conceived a plan for helping the prisoners to escape. Thirty-one of them, led by an Irish mercenary, were involved in the plot. On their daily visits the girls brought in shin-bones of horses and oxen among the food supplies, and these were fashioned by the prisoners into entrenching tools. Laboriously, the men excavated a passage sixty feet long under the prison walls, in constant fear that their tunnel would be discovered by the jailers. But discipline in the prison was lax and silence was rare, since the majority of the prisoners (including four women) were a noisy rabble. Above the hullaballoo nobody heard the sound of the digging. Just as important, nobody discovered the soil and rubble that was being removed, for Anne and Eleanor carried the debris out each day in the baskets and pails used to bring in the food and water.

At length the tunnel reached the outside world and all was ready. The girls informed the prisoners that a sloop was tied up at the quay below the castle. Under cover of darkness, very early one morning in mid-July, thirty-one prisoners scrambled through the tunnel and were led by the girls down to the shore. They all boarded the sloop and captured the crew, only to find that the tide was low and that the vessel was aground. But their luck held. Nearby there was a small yacht that belonged - by a strange quirk of fate - to Lord Cawdor, the man who had been largely responsible for the rapid defeat of the French Invasion force near Fishguard. The little craft was floating freely. After binding the crew of the sloop they took its compass and food supplies and boarded the yacht. Immediately they set sail and were clear of the Pembroke River and out into the Haven before the alarm was raised. Only one of the 31 refugees was recaptured - ironically, he was their leader, an Irishman, who had decided that he had a better chance of returning home if he travelled alone.

Having cleared Milford Haven, the fugitives, still accompanied by Anne and Eleanor, came across a coastal trading brig. This they ran alongside in their heavily laden and overcrowded yacht, waving and shouting that they were shipwrecked sailors in need of help. On boarding her they were surprised to learn that a reward of £500 had already been offered for the two girls, dead or alive. They immediately overpowered the crew and transferred to the larger vessel. The members of the crew, with the exception of the helmsman, were tied up in the hold. Then the empty yacht was cast adrift, eventually to be smashed up by the waves beneath the fierce limestone cliffs of the Castlemartin Peninsula. With the reluctant help of the helmsman a course was set for St Malo, which was reached safely a few days later.

After this nothing is known of the fate of Eleanor and Sergeant Roux. But Anne married her young nobleman shortly after the completion of their exciting adventure, and they came back to Wales to run a public house in the rough, tough industrial town of Merthyr Tydfil. So far as we know, as in all the best love stories, they lived happily every after.

Date : 1797   Sources : Stuart-Jones p.125, Kinross p.91

2.5 The Loss of the Lifeboat "Gem"

The **Gem** was a twelve-oared sailing and pulling lifeboat based at St Justinian's on the edge of Ramsey Sound. It had been based there for 25 years when, on 12th October 1910, it went to the aid of the Barnstaple ketch **Democrat**. The vessel was at anchor in the Sound and was in danger of dragging her anchors during a violent storm; and she was perilously close to the dangerous reef called The Bitches.

Coxwain John Stephens and his crew managed to get alongside the **Democrat** after dark, with the storm increasing all the time from the NNE. They managed to take off the three-man crew of the ketch, but the storm was now so fierce that the oarsmen could not get the lifeboat's bow up against the sea, wind and tide. Inexorably the little vessel was being driven towards The Bitches, so Coxwain Stephens decided to try and run through a narrow passage in the reef. In the pitch darkness he could barely see the gap in the rocks, and as they drove through the wild surf the lifeboat struck a rock and threw all of the lifeboatmen and rescued mariners into the sea. Conditions were so terrible that Coxwain Stephens and two of his men were swept away and drowned. But fifteen others, including the crew of the **Democrat,** managed to scramble onto the wave-swept rocks of The Bitches. The **Gem** drifted away to the south and was smashed up on the cliffs of Ramsey Island.

At the height of the storm nothing could be seen of the terrible events out in the Sound; and indeed nothing was known of the tragedy on the mainland until 9 am the next morning, when one of the castaways managed to attract attention by burning some of his oilskins. There was no sign of the storm abating, and the plight of those on The Bitches looked hopeless, but a young fisherman named Sydney Mortimer, only 18 years old, called for volunteers to go out to the reef. Two of the local coastguards, Sam Guppy and Sam Husk, responded promptly, and all three rushed to Porthclais to launch the **Wave Queen,** a 20-foot rowing boat with a small sail. The boat reached the entrance to the Sound safely, but as soon as it was struck by the full force of the gale most of the rigging was carried away and the boat was half filled with water. Frantically, the men cut away the rest of the rigging, and in fear of their lives baled while every wave threatened to swamp them completely.

But they pressed on with their errand of mercy. Sydney Mortimer kept on rowing, with the steering lines to the rudder tied to his legs, while Guppy and Husk baled for all they were worth. When they approached The Bitches the seas were still too rough for them to approach safely, and the men on the rocks were too weak to be hauled through the water by rope, so the rescuers decided to stand off and wait for the tide to drop. Four hours later young Mortimer took his boat in on the lee side of the reef, took five men off and landed them on Ramsey Island. He then returned and took five more ashore, and was going back for the third time when another mainland boat, manned by Eleazer James and four others, hove into view and took off the remaining survivors.

In the meantime the Fishguard lifeboat **Charterhouse** had been alerted by telegraph, and battled for 16 miles through mountainous seas to help their colleagues in distress. When she arrived in the Sound, all fifteen survivors had been taken off the reef, but the boat belonging to Eleazer

> The vessel was in danger of dragging her anchors during a violent storm.

James was in imminent danger of being swamped, and the lifeboat gave it a line and towed it to safety. All the survivors of the tragedy were then ferried to the mainland, many of them in a state of collapse and in need of urgent medical attention. Later the bodies of Coxwain Stephens and his two crewmen were recovered from the shore of Ramsey Island and brought back to St Justinians.

The tragedy of the **Gem** made a deep and lasting impression on the community of St David's, and the rescuers were showered with honours in recognition of their extraordinary heroism. Sydney Mortimer was of course the hero of the hour; he was awarded the RNLI silver medal together with a cash payment, a Sea Gallantry medal (awarded by King George V at a Buckingham Palace investiture), and a pair of engraved silver binoculars from the Government. But the highest tribute paid to him was that he was appointed coxwain of the St David's Lifeboat, while still only 18 years old, to become the youngest-ever lifeboat coxwain in the British Isles.

Date : 1910   Sources : Goddard p.27, Bennett p.9

2.6 The Hero who did not Sleep

Perhaps the most terrifying episode to affect the town of Pembroke Dock within living memory was "The Great Tanks Fire" which resulted from a German bomb explosion during the Second World War.

The town was an obvious enemy target in view of its military installations, which included a Sunderland flying-boat base, two oil storage depots, and the naval dockyard used as an assembly point for Atlantic convoys. In 1940 and 1941 the town suffered cruelly from enemy bombing raids, with many civilian casualties. On 19 August 1940 a single enemy bomber scored a direct hit on one of the oil storage tanks at Llanreath, and an immense fire raged for 21 days. At first the fire was restricted to one tank and was fought by the local fire service under the control of Mr Arthur Morris, the Pembroke Fire Chief; but as the scale of the fire increased it became apparent that outside help was needed. In due course 650 firemen from twenty-two fire brigades were drafted in to help.

In the early hours of the inferno Fire Chief Morris and his men were able to prevent the burning oil from incinerating hundreds of homes in the nearby streets. But later, as the burning oil roared like a furnace and sent a vast plume of black smoke into the summer sky, the firemen had problems with the water supply. Over the next few days 11 of the 17 tanks caught fire. The firemen worked in almost unbearable heat, often unable to see anything for the acrid black smoke, and drenched in droplets of oil that fell out of the black sky. Many of them collapsed from sheer exhaustion.

Throughout the battle with the burning oil there was one man who did not sleep at all - namely Fire Chief Morris. He remained on his feet directing operations, assessing the changing situation, pulling out exhausted firemen and sending in others, and drafting in new equipment as and when necessary. When he reported to an emergency meeting of Pembroke Borough Council a week after the start of the fire he was unshaven and covered in oil and soot, and the councillors saw that he could hardly keep awake. In the words of a local reporter, "his pale, drawn face told eloquently of the ordeal the men were suffering........ His eyes were heavy and red-rimmed." After the meeting, Arthur Morris returned to the fray.

On 22 August the side of one of the burning tanks burst open and a great spurt of flame engulfed five Cardiff firemen, killing them instantly. On 24 August there was a terrifying "boil over" from one of the tanks, sending a pillar of fire 1,000 feet into the sky and a river of burning oil down the slope towards the town. But as the days passed the inferno was gradually brought under control, with Capt Tom Breakes of the Home Office in overall charge. After a final flare-up the Great Tanks Fire was finally put out on 8th September. Many of the firemen received hospital treatment and in all there were 1,153 casualties in the town. When it was all over Fire Chief Arthur Morris went to bed, and went to sleep.

Afterwards, when the gallantry awards were announced, there was huge local anger that Mr Morris did not receive the George Medal which he so richly deserved, and this anger has persisted to the present day. Nobody knows why he was passed over, but in the dockyard town he is still held in affection as a real "local hero".

Date: 1940   Sources: Richards p 28, Scott p 53

2.7 The Death of John Poyer

John Poyer was the Mayor of Pembroke at the time of the Civil War of 1642-48. He was a staunch Parliamentarian, and together with Colonel Rice Powell and Major-General Rowland Laugharne he was responsible in no small measure for the defeat of the Royalist cause in Pembrokeshire. He sustained the resolve of the town of Pembroke during a Royalist siege in 1644, and provided much support for the Parliamentary military leaders.

But when the first phase of the Civil War ended in 1645 John Poyer and his colleagues were greatly disappointed by the lack of recognition accorded to them by the Parliamentary leaders and by the disbanding of the Roundhead army. In 1648 John Poyer was replaced as mayor, but he refused to give way. He was joined in his rebellion by Powell and Laugharne, and they decided to declare for the Royalists. An army of 8,000 men was raised, and it advanced eastwards through Carmarthenshire and Glamorgan, taking Swansea and Neath on the way. However, the army under Powell and Laugharne was defeated by a highly-trained Parliamentary Army under Horton at St Fagans on 8th May 1648. The two leaders managed to escape, and they fled back to Pembrokeshire. Powell returned to Tenby and Laugharne joined John Poyer in Pembroke.

Now the tragedy began to draw towards its inevitable conclusion. Cromwell had had enough of the insurrection, and he decided on a show of strength in Pembrokeshire. He joined Horton, and together they advanced to Tenby. The old town walls were not strong enough to repel the assault, and the town fell on 31st May. Powell, who had been in charge of the defence of the town, was captured. Cromwell now turned his attention on Pembroke, where Laugharne and Poyer were established with their garrison. Initially, the town walls and powerful defences proved too much for Cromwell, for he had with him only his light artillery. But he decided to starve out the garrison, and he could afford to take his time. He sent to Carmarthenshire for shot to be made in the iron furnaces there, and he ordered his big guns to be sent by sea from Gloucester. Various attempts were made to scale the town walls, but the attackers were repelled on each occasion. At last the big guns arrived, and with adequate new ammunition they opened fire on 11th July. After a seven-week siege Poyer was forced to surrender, and he and Major-General Laugharne joined Powell in captivity.

The three renegades were taken to London, where they were tried by a court-martial and sentenced to death. As a gesture of clemency Cromwell decided that only one of them should die. According to legend they were asked to draw lots, but they refused. So three slips of paper were given to a child. One of the slips was blank, and the other two carried the words "Life given by God". The child gave a slip to each of the prisoners. Mayor John Poyer, who had served his people and the Parliamentary cause so well, received the blank one. He was shot at Covent Garden by a firing-squad, having faced his executioners with courage and dignity.

Date : 1648 *Sources : Leach p.211, Miles p.176*

PEMBROKESHIRE FOLK TALES

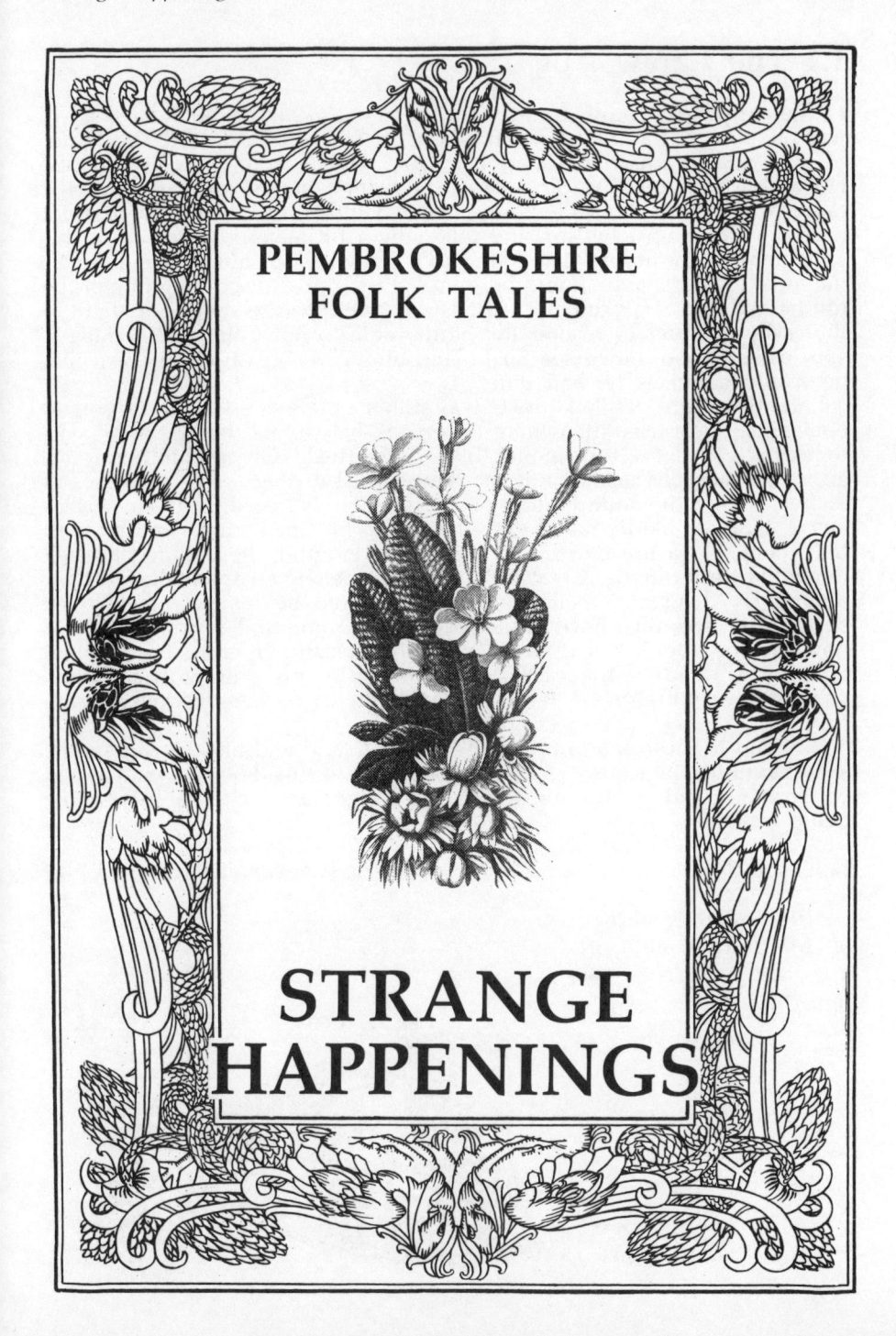

STRANGE HAPPENINGS

3.1 The Carew Ape

In the early seventeenth century the immensely wicked Sir Roland Rhys was the occupant and lord of Carew Castle. His son seduced the daughter of a Flemish tradesman called Horwitz, who was one of his tenants. Horwitz was tended by Sir Roland's servants, but he turned up at the castle to complain about the young man's conduct, but the lord would not hear a word against his son and following a furious argument he set his tame ape on the unfortunate man. Poor Horwitz was almost dead before the lord called his ape off and he then led the brute away, laughing at the fun he had had at his tenant's expense. Horwitz had to spend the night in the castle in order to recuperate; hardly able to move because of fatigue and loss of blood, he cursed Sir Roland under his breath and prayed that he would suffer as he had done.

Later that night, while Horwitz was still in a state of shock and trying to obtain some rest from the pain of his ordeal, he was startled out of his wits to hear screams of terror echoing through the castle. On and on they went, growing gradually weaker and changing at last to great sobs and gasps of distress. Then the sounds died out altogether. Petrified by what he had heard, Horwitz hardly dared move, but then he smelt smoke and realized that there was a fire burning in the castle. Painfully he dragged himself down the steps into the Great Hall, where he beheld an appalling sight. Sir Roland lay dead in a pool of blood, mutilated by his pet ape. In the struggle the ape must have dislodged some burning timber in the fire, and now the ape, too, lay dead in the midst of a blazing inferno. The terrified tenant staggered to the castle gate and made his painful way home, vowing never to return. A large portion of the castle was destroyed in the fire.

It is said that the shadowy figures of Sir Roland and his ape can still be seen haunting the ruins of Carew Castle, and to this day local people talk of terrible sounds disturbing the dead of night and echoing around the castle walls.

Date : c 1603 ?   Sources : Warner p.65, Underwood p.48

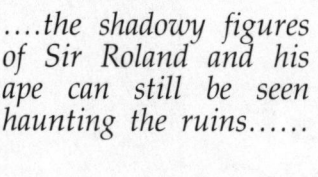

....the shadowy figures of Sir Roland and his ape can still be seen haunting the ruins......

3.2 Trouble at Tafarn Newydd

Once upon a time (in 1980, to be precise) an English couple took over the running of the New Inn, Tafarn Newydd, on the main road not far from Rosebush. The inn is a famous one, long established as a coaching inn and representing the "last stop before the Presely Hills" for those travelling from Haverfordwest to Cardigan. For centuries it has also been a popular hostelry for local people from the surrounding farming area in the Presely foothills.

In 1980 business was a little slack, and the new owners decided that some positive action was needed in order to build up trade. Accordingly they introduced a Saturday night striptease act, and also topless barmaids, since in faraway England such things were all the rage. However, the hapless owners had not fully appreciated the nature of the community into which they had moved, and they did not anticipate the nature of the local reaction. Very quickly their local trade dropped right off, as did visits by holidaymakers with young families. They also found themselves shunned by most of their Welsh neighbours, and did not realise that they had caused grave offence to the strong nonconformist religious traditions of the area.

Relations with the locals went from bad to worse, and even the most hardened of the regulars, who had drunk at Tafarn Newydd for decades, began to drift away. The publican and his wife felt aggrieved, since they knew that the average Welsh farmer enjoyed the sight of a topless barmaid as much as the next man. The barmaids continued to display their talents, and as time went on lost local trade was replaced by trade from further afield. Legend has it that furtive gentlemen from as far away as Haverfordwest and Milford Haven began to frequent the pub, and loud young men riding motor-bikes and wearing black leathers began to appear regularly from Llanelli and Swansea.

Suddenly, one night in May 1983, Tafarn Newydd went up in flames. The blazing inferno was seen from miles around, and by the time the fire brigade arrived there was nothing they could do to save the building. By morning the inn was reduced to a blackened shell, with nothing but its four ancient outside walls still standing. Daubed onto the front wall were the words "Busty Berta was 'ere" and "This was an English family home". Thankfully, nobody was hurt in the blaze. The landlord and his wife were away on holiday in Majorca at the time, and the initial impression was of course that this was a straightforward example of arson by Welsh language extremists directed towards an English immigrant family which had upset local sensibilities.

But then there came a final twist to the story. Police and fire brigade experts who examined the gutted building considered the scale of the destruction too large for comfort; locals told of the landlord and his wife broadcasting the news of their foreign holiday rather too loudly around the community; others told of the wife setting off for her holiday in the sun carrying her fur coat with her; and in due course an insurance claim for £155,000 was stopped by the insurance company "pending further investigations". Eventually the couple were arrested by the police and charged with making a false insurance claim. At the same time a friend of the family was charged with arson. At the trial in Swansea Crown Court in 1984 the landlord and the accomplice who had set the building on fire were found guilty and sent to prison for 12 months.

For some years after the fire Tafarn Newydd stood as a forlorn empty shell. Now, however, it has been rebuilt and restored, and is back in business, providing traditional refreshment for travellers and locals alike. Needless to say, Berta and the topless barmaids have passed into the realm of fairytale and legend.

Date : 1983   *Sources : newspaper cuttings*

3.3 The Nevern Cuckoo

April 7th is St Brynach's Day, and every year as far back as folk could remember it was the day when the first cuckoo of Spring arrived at Nevern and perched on the tall Celtic cross outside the church. It was thought that this was something of a religious duty among cuckoos, for St Brynach, just like St Francis of Assisi, had had a special understanding of animals. So the cuckoo came as God's messenger of rebirth and renewal, and it became the custom that the priest of Nevern should not say Mass on St Brynach's day until the cuckoo had arrived.

One year there was a hard, long winter and when April 7th came there was no sign of Spring. The ground was still frozen and there were no spring flowers and no buds on the trees. All the same, the people of Nevern gathered outside the church to await the arrival of the messenger. For hour after hour they waited, stamping their feet and blowing on their cold hands in order to keep warm. Midday came and went, and the throng became chilled and weary. Some of the congregation wanted to go home, and some urged the priest to go into the church and celebrate Mass without further delay. But the priest would not yield, saying "God cares for all his creatures, and he will neither disappoint us nor let the cuckoo fail".

The afternoon light was fading into a cold twilight when suddenly the assembled people heard a faint fluttering between the ancient bleeding yews which lined the path from the church gate to the church door. God's messenger had arrived. The tired cuckoo alighted unsteadily on top of St Brynach's cross and uttered the first "cuckoo" of Spring. Gratefully, the priest and his people gave brief thanks to God and hurried into the church to celebrate their much-delayed Mass.

When they came out they found a dead cuckoo at the foot of the ornate stone cross. The terrible journey across the snow-covered mountains of Europe and the storm-lashed Channel had been too much for it. But it had kept its trust.

Date : c 1500   *Sources : Styles p.35, Roberts p.10, Parry-Jones p.153*

3.4 The Last Invasion of Britain

The Last Invasion of Britain was an historical event of great national importance, but it has also become a piece of local folk-lore. The somewhat farcical story of the French invasion force which landed not far from Goodwick has all the ingredients of a good story, and indeed the tale has been passed on by word of mouth from generation to generation over a period of almost 200 years.

In 1797 Britain was at war with revolutionary France. The British government was concerned lest the French should mount an invasion, and the French believed that it was possible to promote rebellion among the disenchanted poor people who lived and worked on the land. Accordingly a French invasion force of about 1500 convicts and mercenaries was despatched under the command of the American General Tate. There were four vessels in the expeditionary force, and Tate had instructions to land most of his troops on the coast of Ireland with a smaller force to be put ashore either at Bristol or on the shore of Cardigan Bay. However, a combination of muddled instructions, poor planning and unfavourable winds caused the four vessels to round St David's Head together under full sail on the morning of 22nd February.

The vessels were sighted and recognized as French naval ships by Thomas Williams of Treleddyn Farm, and he rode along the coast road towards Fishguard, keeping the vessels in view and raising the alarm as he passed through one hamlet after another. The news of the invasion forces travelled fast. By the time the vessels reached Fishguard Bay the locals were expecting them. Tate attempted a landing at Fishguard, but one blank shot from Fishguard Fort convinced him that there was an armed garrison ashore, and so he retreated back out to sea. This was just as well, since the fort had no ammunition at all, and the garrison was in a state of total disarray!

The day was uncommonly hot for the time of year, and the sea was calm, so Tate and the naval commander Castagnier (who wanted to get rid of his disreputable passengers and return to France) decided to put the troops and supplies ashore immediately. Out of sight of the town of Fishguard, and under the guidance of one James Bowen (a local man convicted of horse-stealing and pressed into service in France as a mercenary) Carregwastad Point was selected as the landing place. The first troops went ashore on the low rocky ledges of the headland at 5 pm, and the operation continued during a calm moonlit night. By morning all the troops and supplies had been ferried ashore. Tate established his headquarters at Trehowel Farm; Castagnier and his ships left for home; and French troops took control of Carnwnda Rocks, the highest point in the area. Meanwhile, the local military leadership was in a state of panic, since there was no organized body of troops to oppose the French and a shortage of arms and ammunition.

If only the French had pressed home their advantage things might have turned out differently; but the invasion rapidly degenerated into farce. Tate was remorseful at his involvement in the affair, and his officers were rebellious and resentful that they had been abandoned by Castagnier in a strange and hostile land. The "troops" were undisciplined and rowdy, and ranged far and wide looting, stealing food and killing farm animals. In isolated incidents throughout Pencaer the invaders encountered hostility and active opposition; there was never the slightest chance that they would activate a "peasants revolt". As luck would have it, a Portuguese trading vessel had gone aground in the vicinity a month or so earlier, and there were plentiful supplies of Portuguese wine in all the local farms and cottages. As Thursday 23rd February wore on, more and more of the men (and their officers) became drunk, and by the evening every semblance of discipline had disappeared.

Meanwhile one of the local gentry, Lord Cawdor, had assumed command of a mottley assortment of 575 local militiamen. The "army" was made up of Lord Cawdor's own Yeomanry Cavalry, the Cardigan Militia, the Fishguard Fencibles, the Pembroke Volunteers, and a party of Royal Navy sailors. Having almost walked into a French ambush at Manorowen Lord Cawdor withdrew to Fishguard for the night. There were no proper military engagements, but legend has it that a group of Welsh women, in their traditional flannel costumes and tall hats, paraded round and round a hill near Fishguard, giving Tate's officers the impression from a distance that an endless line of troops was marching in to reinforce the local garrison. Whether this was a deliberate ploy on Lord Cawdor's part, or simply an accident of fate, has never been satisfactorily resolved; but whatever the truth of the matter Tate decided to surrender after less that 24 hours ashore.

The first surrender note was sternly rejected by Lord Cawdor, but French officers signed the surrender terms in the Royal Oak Inn in Fishguard on the morning of Friday 24th February, and Tate's signature was added later at Trehowel Farm. During the day groups of French soldiers were rounded up in various parts of Pencaer. Many local people were involved in the action, including "the Welsh heroine" Jemima Nicholas, who captured twelve Frenchmen single-handed and armed only with a pitchfork, in a field near Llanwnda. Later, when asked how she had managed this heroic feat, she simply replied "I surrounded them!" A hundred years after the invasion a memorial stone was erected to Jemima Nicholas against the wall of St Mary's Church, Fishguard.

The French troops laid down their arms on Goodwick Sands on the afternoon of 24th February, less 25 who were too drunk or otherwise too incapable to attend the ceremony. All the troops were then marched to Haverfordwest under guard, where they were imprisoned in the castle and in the churches of St Mary, St Martin and St Thomas. The great invasion was over. The real hero was Lord Cawdor, who had shown great determination and leadership in difficult circumstances. The Pembrokeshire Yeomanry later received the only battle honour ever awarded to a British Army unit for service on its own soil. But it has to be said that in spite of the heroic efforts of Lord Cawdor, Jemima Nicholas and assorted Welsh ladies in tall hats, the French invasion of 1797 involved more farce than force.......

Date : 1797   *Sources : Kinross, Stuart-Jones, Roberts p.16*

3.5 The Lost Child of Pwll and Rhiannon

Pwll, Prince of Dyfed and Lord of its Seven Regions, had his palace at Narberth and lived there happily with his wife Rhiannon. He loved her dearly, for she was the kindest and most gentle of women, besides being the most beautiful in all of Dyfed.

When a son was born to Pwll and Rhiannon there was great rejoicing, and six nursemaids were appointed to keep a constant watch on the baby. But they became drowsy, and while they slept the boy disappeared. Fearful that they would be punished for betraying their trust, they decided to place the blame on the gentle Rhiannon. Accordingly they killed a puppy and smeared its blood all over the baby's nursery. Then they went to Rhiannon and smeared blood on her hands and face. They told Pwll and the court that she had killed the child and had struggled violently when they tried to subdue her. Their story was believed, even by the wise men of Dyfed.

Pwll would not believe that Rhiannon had killed the baby, and he would not have her put away. But the wise men decreed that she was guilty, and devised a penance for her. She had to remain in the palace of Narberth for seven years, beside the mounting-block near the main gate; and there she should relate her story to all who came by, and offer to carry every visitor on her back into the palace.

While Rhiannon had been giving birth to her son in Narberth, strange things had been happening in Gwent, far away in the eastern corner of Wales. The Lord of Gwent was Teyrnon, who owned the best mare in the world. Every May Eve the mare gave birth to a foal, which immediately vanished. But Teyrnon decided to do something about it, and on this particular May Eve had brought the mare to the palace and kept watch on it. The mare gave birth to a fine colt, but at once Teyrnon heard a great noise like a storm, with a choir of wailing voices into the bargain. Then the huge arm of a monster came through the window and seized the newborn colt. But Teyrnon was ready for it. Quick as a flash he seized his sword and cut off the arm at the elbow. There was a fearsome roar, and Teyrnon rushed outside to see if he could catch sight of the creature. But it was too dark to see anything. When he returned he was amazed to see an infant boy in swaddling clothes in the straw next to the frightened colt.

The Lord of Gwent and his wife decided to rear the mysterious child as their own, and christened him Gwri Gwallt Euryn (gold haired boy). The lad with the golden hair thrived and grew strong, thrived and grew strong, and on his fourth birthday they gave him the colt that had been born on the same night as himself. Then the foster-parents heard from a traveller the sad story of Rhiannon. Teyrnon looked hard at the boy, and remembering the face of Pwll from the time they had spent together in days gone by, he realised that Gwri must be Pwll's missing son. He discussed matters with his wife, and they decided to return the boy to his real parents so that Rhiannon's terrible ordeal could be brought to an end.

So they set off for Narberth, with little Gwri riding on his own horse. When they arrived they saw Rhiannon standing near the main gate. She greeted them, but they refused to hear her story or to be carried on her back. They went into the palace, where Pwll had prepared a magnificent feast for them. Teyrnon took the boy by the hand and set him before Pwll,

The lad with the golden hair thrived and grew strong...

and told the story of his discovery and his childhood in Gwent. All those present, including the wise men of Dyfed, agreed that the likeness between Pwll and Gwri was so striking that they could only be father and son.

Then Rhiannon was declared free of any guilt. Her penance was lifted from her and she was immediately restored to her position of honour at the right hand of the Prince of Dyfed. The boy with the golden hair was given the name his mother had given him when he was born - Pryderi, which means Anxiety. Teyrnon and his wife returned to their own country, refusing the gifts offered by Pwll and accepting only his offer of support and faithful friendship. And so the family was reunited in love and harmony, and Pryderi grew up to be a great Lord of Dyfed after his father.

Date : c 1050 ?   Sources : Bowen p.26, G. Jones p.13, Webb p.21

3.6 St Teilo's Skull

Once upon a time there was a famous holy well near Llandeilo Farm, not far from Maenclochog. As the name implies the well was associated with St Teilo, and it had miraculous healing powers. But the healing was not simply associated with the waters of the well, for those who sought relief from their ailments were required by custom to drink the waters from the skull of the saint himself.

According to tradition Teilo had a favourite maid, and on his deathbed he charged her to take his skull, twelve months from the day of his burial, from Llandeilo Fawr in Carmarthenshire to his native church in Pembrokeshire. This the girl did, and the skull came into the possession of the Melchior family of Llandeilo, who looked after it from generation to generation. It was part of the ritual that all who came for healing should be handed the skull containing the holy water by a person born in Llandeilo Farm. The Melchiors, over the centuries, charged nothing for their service, nor did they believe in the efficacy of the skull or the well, but many who came were healed.

One tale is told of a man who brought his son to St Teilo's Well all the way from Glamorgan for healing, but they returned home none the better for the long journey. Then the father remembered that the boy had not actually drunk the water from the skull. They repeated the long journey, the son drank the water as prescribed, and was immediately healed.

Nobody knows where the skull is today. It was sold in 1927 for £50 by Miss Melchior, the last of the family, who mistakenly believed she was selling it to Llandaff Cathedral. But by that time medical science had arrived; few people believed in the power of the skull, and hardly any sick people came to be healed. And in any case, Rev Baring Gould had examined the skull and declared it to have been that of a young woman. Now the church is in ruins and the well is used simply to supply water to a nearby farm.

Date : c 1500 ?   *Sources : Rhys p.399, Parry-Jones p.123, Miles p.196*

3.7 Cecil Longshanks and the Toads

The farm of Trellyffaint, near Nevern, has been in existence for well over a thousand years. Once upon a time a young man called Cecil Longshanks lived there. He happened to fall ill, upon which he became persecuted by a plague of toads. At first he was simply irritated by them, but as the toads grew in number he became very angry. More and more toads appeared, and his anger turned to fear. Eventually he became quite terrified. His friends tried to help by killing as many of the creatures as they could, but the toads simply increased at a frightening rate. At last, exhausted by their efforts, Cecil's friends decided to haul him up in a large bag into a high tree which they reckoned would be out of reach of the toads. But poor Cecil could not escape from the pestilence; thousands and thousands of toads climbed up the tree, eating all the foliage and bark and eventually finding their way into the bag. Then they consumed Cecil as well, leaving nothing behind but a sackful of white bones which rattled as it moved in the warm summer breeze.

Date : c 1150 ?   Sources : Giraldus p.170, Roberts p.12

3.8 Message from India

In Manordeifi Church, close to the banks of the River Teifi near Llechryd, there is a memorial to a young British army soldier who died on active duty in India under mysterious circumstances. The story goes that in due course the Army shipped back a large and oddly-shaped box for burial. It didn't smell too good when it arrived at Llechryd, and on opening it up the soldier's family discovered an extremely large and partly decomposed tiger inside. A telegraph signal was sent off to India to ask whether some mistake had been made, and to insist that the body of the young man should be returned to the family post haste. Back came the reply from foreign parts, short and to the point:
    "Tiger in box. Sahib in tiger."

Date : c 1920 ?   Source : Worsley p.62

3.9 Harvest Time on Trevalen Downs

One bright morning in early spring a farmer was sowing barley seed on the rich limestone soils of Trevalen Downs not far from St Govan's Chapel. As he cast his seed to right and left he noticed a tall, dignified stranger watching him. When he approached the stranger asked what he was doing. "Sowing barley", replied the farmer. "But", said the stranger, "this seed which you are sowing will decay in the ground". The farmer replied with confidence "Yes, it will. But it will burst into life again, and grow, and at harvest time I will gather it."
Then the tall stranger looked the farmer in the eye and challenged him. "Do you believe", he asked, "that that which is dead can come to life?" "I do", replied the farmer. "Then go home", said the stranger quietly, "and get thy sickle and cut thy corn. For I am the Resurrection and the Life."
The farmer thought this very strange, but nonetheless he obeyed the instruction and set off for home in order to fetch his sickle. But as he hurried away the tall stranger said "If any should come to this place seeking after me, and should ask if I have passed this way, you shall say unto them that you have indeed seen me, but in sowing time."
Later, when the farmer came back to his barley field the stranger had gone. But the barley was ripe for harvesting - on the very same day that it had been sown. The farmer set to work with his sickle, and suddenly noticed an approaching band of ruffians. They accosted him rudely, and asked if a tall stranger had passed that way. The farmer replied as he had been instructed. The men gave up the chase in despair, then turned and returned the way that they had come.
Later the farmer discovered that the tall stranger had been hiding in the crevice behind the altar of nearby St Govan's Chapel. He saw that the rock had miraculously opened up to receive him, and that his impression had been imprinted upon the solid rock. And those who visit the little chapel can still see this impression to this day.

Date : c 1750 ?   Source : Roberts p.30

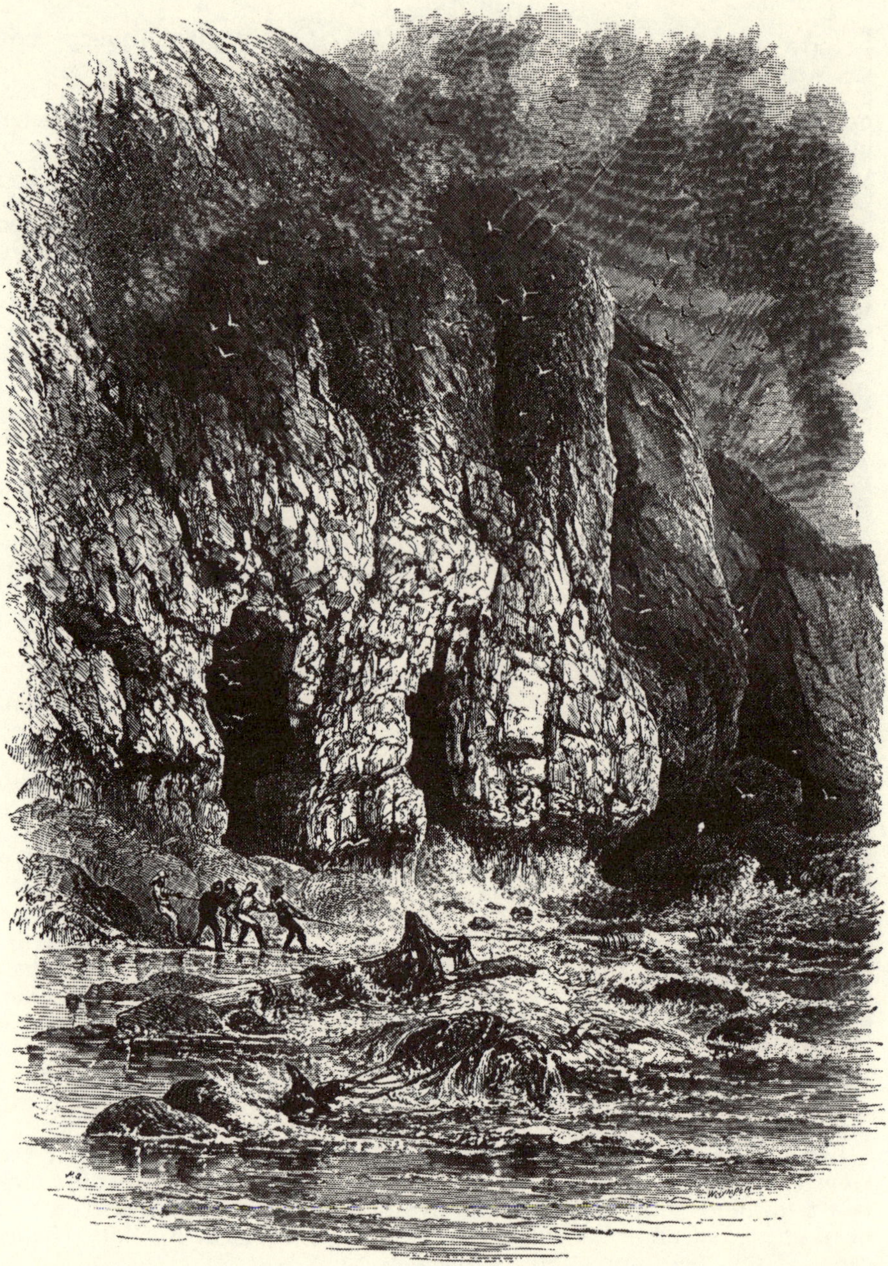

3.10 Explosion at Druidston

In 1791 the Scarborough vessel **Increase,** heavily laden with a cargo of Government stores (including gunpowder and ordnance) ran ashore in a storm at Druidston Haven. Local people had seen it in distress out in St Bride's Bay, and followed its progress as it was driven ashore; so that by the time it reached the shore there was a large crowd waiting for it.

Some of the locals, being "the very lowest order of the community", were more interested in plundering the wreck than saving the shipwrecked mariners, and as soon as the tide had fallen sufficiently they swarmed all over the battered vessel. There must have been more than a hundred of them, working in groups, squabbling over items discovered on board, and even coming to blows over the possession of the more valuable items. Some worked on board the vessel and others on the rocks and on the beach. A considerable quantity of gunpowder in barrels was passed down onto the rocks, but many items of plunder were simply thrown down to be grabbed by the willing hands beneath. Most of the men were on the ship and most of the women down below. Some hauled on ropes and others hurried back and forth across the beach with their ill-gotten gains before the tide came in again and caused further damage to the wreck.

Before long a good quantity of gunpowder had been taken from the hold. However, many of the casks had been damaged as the ship drove onto the rocks, and the deadly powder was accidentally scattered onto the rocks and sandy beach. Then one of the wreckers on the deck of the ship shouted down to his colleagues that he would throw down quite enough plunder to satisfy everybody, and flung down a musket to one of his friends. The friend failed to catch it, and it glanced off a rock. The spark which resulted caused a huge explosion, and the sand and rocks were enveloped in fire and smoke. Eight people were killed instantly, and afterwards their bodies were so badly damaged that they could not be identified. Sixty others were terribly injured, and many of them later died lingering deaths as a result of their burns. Ironically, the women on the rocks suffered most, for their long skirts went up in flames, causing severe burns which disfigured them for life. Afterwards, the Pembrokeshire gentry, who professed to be violently opposed to the wrecking activities of the peasantry, said that the Druidston explosion was divine retribution for the greed and inhumanity of all those involved.

Date : 1791   Sources : Miles p.107, Brinton & Worsley p.74

Opposite:
Some hauled on ropes and others hurried back and forth across the beach with their ill-gotten gains before the tide came in again and caused further damage to the wreck.

3.11 Visit from a Viking

In 1934 the village of Monkton was visited by a tall young man from Stockholm with the name of Nordin. He was a medical student. On a visit to the Vicar he related that in a previous incarnation he had been born in Monkton of Viking parents, more than 1,000 years earlier. The Vicar was somewhat sceptical, but he took Mr Nordin to the top of the church tower, where the young man pointed out the locations of ancient walls which nobody in the neighbourhood knew about. On investigation, the Vicar later discovered these old walls. The young man also recognized the Old Hall at Monkton, told the Vicar where and how it had been altered over the years, and recalled that in his previous life it had been a nunnery. The Vicar had not previously been aware of this, but it helped him to explain a number of strange events in the Old Hall (then used as a vicarage) including a heavy knocking on his bedroom door every morning at four o'clock, which he assumed must have been a ghostly continuation of the call to early morning devotions. Upon later research the vicar also confirmed the young man's description of the original outline of the building.

Date : 1934   *Source : Bielski, p.43*

3.12 The Fall of Picton Castle

Sir Richard Philipps of Picton Castle was at the time of the Civil War a staunch Parliamentarian, although like most of the other Pembrokeshire gentry he was not averse to changing sides when it suited him. In 1644 the castle was garrisoned for Parliament, at a time when the Royalist troops were making a determined assault on South Pembrokeshire.

One of the bastions of the castle housed the nursery on the ground floor. Sir Richard's small son Erasmus was normally looked after by a nursemaid since he was only one year old at the time. The nursery had a single small window, which opened onto the garden. One hot day in the month of July the window was wide open and the nursemaid was standing at the window with the child in her arms. It so happened that a trooper from the Royalist Army approached the castle on horseback in order to deliver a letter to Sir Richard, and on seeing the maid at the window he called to her to take the letter and to deliver it to her master. This the girl agreed to do, and the trooper approached with the letter in his hand. The maid stretched forward to receive the envelope, still holding the baby to her breast. Suddenly the trooper realised that he was being presented with an opportunity too good to miss, so he grabbed the baby from the maid and immediately threatened to kill him with his sword if the castle was not surrendered to the Royalist cause.

The terrified nursemaid rushed to her master and pleaded that he should save the baby. Of course Sir Richard had no option but to secure the release of his child, and the castle was duly surrendered to the King's troop as demanded by the soldier.
Fate decreed that this wicked deed should not be rewarded, and in fact the castle was held for only a few months before it was re-taken by Parliamentary forces under Col Rowland Laugharne in October 1645.

Date : 1645   *Source : Laws p.329*

3.13 The Mermaid at Aberbach

Treseissyllt is a large farm not far from the beach of Aberbach in North Pembrokeshire. One fine summer's morning, very early, the farmer went down to the beach, and there he was surprised to see a *gwenhudwy* (mermaid) on the shingle bank, apparently stranded by the retreating tide. She was, like all mermaids, extremely beautiful, with long golden hair; and the farmer, being young and lusty, grabbed her quick as a flash. Without further ado he carried her, thrashing about wildly, up to the farm. There he placed her in the bathtub, with a good supply of salt water to keep her moist. The poor girl pleaded tearfully to be returned to the ocean, but the farmer simply replied that he had other plans for her, and refused to let her go.
At last the mermaid became angry, and after pleading again, without success, to be set free she put a curse *(cyfaredd)* upon the farm. Never again, she said, would a child be born there because of the farmer's wickedness. Now it was the farmer's turn to become alarmed, and in an attempt to right the wrong he had done he at last returned the mermaid to the sea.
But it was too late. For more than a hundred years the curse hung over the heads of the farmers of Treseissyllt, and no children were born there. But the curse brought with it certain compensations. One old farmer who sold the farm to a younger man said as he left "Duw, duw, you are indeed a lucky man". The young farmer asked why this should be. With a twinkle in his eye the old man replied "It is said that no child will ever again be born at Treseissyllt. Just think what that means, with all those pretty servant girls lodging beneath your roof!"

Date : c 1820   *Source : Roberts p.9*

3.14 The Missing Falcon Chicks

Some years ago, Pembrokeshire's few remaining pairs of peregrine falcons were struggling for survival. There were many thefts of eggs and chicks from falcon nests on the cliffs, and members of the Dyfed Wildlife Trust and the RSPB kept a constant watch on the most vulnerable nest sites during the nesting season in order to frighten off would-be nest robbers.

One such nest on the north coast near Newport was being watched night and day by Trust members. One member left for home at the end of his shift, having ascertained that the two chicks in the nest were safe. But when his colleague arrived after a little while the chicks had gone. Clearly somebody must have had not only the nest but also the nest-watchers under surveillance. He had got at the chicks as soon as the way was clear, and had made his escape, probably aided by at least one accomplice.

The alarm was immediately raised, and the police were informed of the theft. They swung into action at once, and soon there were road blocks throughout the area, while Trust members scoured the fields, footpaths and lanes near the nest site. But there was no sign anywhere of the criminals.

At last somebody had a bright idea. There was, apparently, a meeting of diviners going on at that very moment in St Dogmaels, and it was thought that they might be able to help. So they were enlisted to the cause, and willingly agreed to see what they could do. They got out their maps and pendulums, and put their heads together. At last a message came to the police. The diviners had seen a sign, and they suggested that a red Fiat car travelling on the A40 towards St Clears with two passengers should be stopped and searched. Accordingly a road block was set up, and sure enough, along came a red Fiat with two men inside. They were acting very suspiciously, and were most reluctant to open the boot of their car when asked to do so by the police.

At last the men opened the boot of the car - to reveal net, lamp, gaff and two gleaming salmon freshly poached from the River Teifi. The men were duly arrested and charged with poaching. Later, the St Dogmaels diviners apologised to the police for their lack of precision - they had all agreed that there was something fishy about the red Fiat, but they had, from a distance of 30 miles or so, been unable to discern exactly what the boot of the car contained. Ironically, it turned out that the Falcon chicks had not been stolen at all; they had left the nest of their own accord, and had flown a little way down the cliff under the supervision of their mother.

Date : c 1982   *Source : word of mouth*

3.15 Mererid, the Guardian of the Sacred Well

Once upon a time, **very** long ago, there was a fine fertile kingdom which later came to be called Cantre'r Gwaelod or the Lowland Hundred, to the north of Dewisland and Cemais. However, the land was known to its people and to neighbouring peoples as Maes Gwyddno. As one might expect from the name, it belonged to a king called Gwyddno, and there were many fine palaces, and many princes and warriors who lived there in those far-off times.

There were four particularly famous warriors, named Mor, Kynran, Kenedyr, and Seithennin. The mightiest and wisest of these was Mor, who was nicknamed Mor the Grand because of his feats in battle. Kynran was thought by many to be weak in the head. He was valiant in battle, but he was liable to strange utterances, predicting over and over again that the waters were going to burst forth, that the land would be lost beneath a great flood, and that the people should build boats in order to save themselves. Nobody took his seriously, for the sea was far away, and between Gwyddno's kingdom and the far-off land of Ireland there was a fertile plain with two slow and gentle rivers flowing to the south-western ocean. Kenedyr trusted nobody and was always prepared for war; he built himself a fine fort, called in Welsh Caer Kenedyr, to protect himself and his clan at times of trouble. And Seithennin, the last of the four, was himself a son of a king of Dyfed called Plaws Hen. He was honest and faithful to King Gwyddno, but he was over-fond of wine and mead and was of somewhat feeble mind.

In the kingdom of Gwyddno there was a magic well, whose secrets were entrusted to a damsel called Mererid. She did not herself know these secrets, for they were tabu to all but the high priests. Mererid knew only that the well contained the mysteries of wisdom, and inspiration, and poetry; and she knew that nobody was allowed to gaze into its depths. Only she was allowed to take the sacred water from the well while averting her eyes, and only she could serve it in golden goblets to the king and his nobles. It was also her duty to keep the well covered with a flat stone to contain its secrets and to keep it from overflowing. She was a mysterious and very beautiful young woman, well versed in the ways of the spirits. Like the priests of the kingdom, she was given to wierd incantations and strange behaviour which the common people did not understand. Indeed, Mererid was herself a sort of priestess, and even the king, while thinking her very comely, was slightly in awe of her.

Now it happened that the king had been at war with one of the kings of Ireland who had coveted his territory; but he had won a mighty victory and returned to Maes Gwyddno bearing with him the severed head of the Irish king. Flanked by his heroes Mor, Kenedyr, Kynran and Seithennin he rode through the gates of his fortified town to a tumultuous welcome from the people. The king and his people rejoiced. There was singing and dancing in the streets, the priests offered thanks to the gods, and in the king's palace a great feast was prepared.

The feasting and celebrations went on far into the night, with music and entertainments of the most lavish kind. The wine flowed freely, and everybody drank too much. Mererid was invited to the party, and temporarily forgot her sacred duties to join in the jollification. She became a centre of attention, because she had never before been seen to let her hair down; and she too drank too much wine......

In the early hours Mererid returned to her well, none too steady on her feet and singing to herself in the moonlit velvet darkness. She thought that all was well with the world. Then she had an idea. No harm would be done, she thought, if she was to remove the stone cover from the sacred well and to take just a little peep inside. Perhaps she could obtain a glimpse of its secrets. Perhaps she would discover something of its wisdom and inspiration, and maybe write a poem or two to celebrate the king's victory in battle. And, so, feeling a trifle afraid but giggling to herself nonetheless, she moved the heavy stone aside and gazed into the depths of the well.

Immediately a great flood of water burst out of the well and threatened to overwhelm Mererid. She screamed and attempted to replace the stone cover, but the torrent continued, and in her drunken state her struggles with the heavy stone were clumsy and to no avail. At last she gave up the fight and fled from the well, shouting out warning at the top of her voice. But nobody heard her, for the common people were all deeply asleep following their celebrations, and the king and his family and nobles were still making merry in the palace. Inexorably the water poured out of the well and followed Mererid in a great tidal wave, flooding the town and the wide fertile plains of the kingdom. She struggled up to the highest rocky crag in the town and there, as she watched the water rising higher and higher, she threw her arms wide open and cried and pleaded and offered prayers to her gods for deliverance and forgiveness.

But those were hard times, and the gods would not be denied their retribution. As the waters rose many hundreds of townspeople, and many hundreds more in the countryside of Maes Gwyddno, were drowned. The floods swept through the palace, carrying away King Gwyddno, his wife and his nobles. And Mererid, on the summit crag, was the last to drown, weeping bitterly as the flood waters closed over her.

Only three men survived the drowning of the Lowland Hundred. One of them was called Kynran, who had prophesied that one day this disaster would happen. And he it was that had prepared a boat for which others had ridiculed him, and in which he floated away to the higher lands of Cemais. Another survivor was a bard who later composed a lament for the lost land and for the drowned king and his heroic warriors. The lament was remembered and repeated thousands of times by generation after generation of bards. And at last it was written down and included as one of the ancient manuscripts which came to be known collectively as the **Black Book of Carmarthen**. Mererid is still remembered as the bringer of catastrophe, through trying to know that which should remain unknown; and the well still holds its secret to this day, deep down beneath the grey silty waters of Cardigan Bay.

Date: c 200 BC ?   *Source: Rhys, p. 383*

3.16 The Wreckers of Marros

Early in the eighteenth century, on the hills above Marros Sands, there was an isolated smallholding where a farmer, his wife and a teenage son scraped a poor living from the soil. Times were hard, and after two years of harvest failures and disease among the cattle the son could stand it no longer. He left home and went to sea, seeking fortune and adventure. The fields were neglected and the animals provided little milk or meat, and the farmer and his wife became bitter and disillusioned.

After a while, in a desperate attempt to survive, the couple joined a gang of wreckers who operated on the coast between Pendine and Amroth. Night after night they placed false lights on the cliffs, luring merchant ships to their doom on the treacherous sands of Telpin and Marros. The beach became a graveyard for coastal trading vessels. Many sailors died, but the couple prospered, and before long they enjoyed good wine, good food and fine clothes.

One morning, after yet another cargo ship had foundered on the sands and broken up in the wild surf, the couple were collecting boxes of cargo from the beach below their farm. They came across a seaman, face down in the sand. He was still alive, and following the practice of the wreckers they despatched him by crushing his skull with a heavy stone. They dragged the body up the beach and began to remove the gold rings from the lifeless fingers. Too late, the wife realised that she recognized one of the rings. They turned the body over, and recognized the features of their own son.

It is said that from that day on no light was ever seen around the farmhouse on the hill above Marros. The farmer and his wife spent the rest of their lives weighed down with their terrible secret and afflicted by endless nightmares.

Date : c 1720 ?   Source : Radford p.33

The beach became a graveyard for coastal trading vessels.

3.17 Vision at Treffgarne

In the late eighteenth century a farmer's wife named Sarah Evans was renowed as a *dewin* (soothsayer) who had the ability to foresee future events. She was in all other respects a perfectly normal farmer's wife, one of the Bevan family of Market Mill and now living quietly with her husband at Penyfeidr not far from Treffgarne Rocks.

From the slopes above the farm there was a fine view down into the spectacular and thickly-wooded Treffgarne Gorge, at one time renowned as a haunt of highwaymen and thieves and still regarded, in the eighteenth century, as a place very difficult of access. One day, around the year 1770, Sarah came in to the house and described to her husband a most remarkable sight which she had seen in the gorge. Apparently she had watched a large number of heavily laden wagons or carts going very fast, one after another in a straight line, but with no oxen or horses pulling them. As if this was not strange enough, the first of the wagons had smoke coming out of it, as if it was on fire. She could not explain the vision, and neither could her husband.

Sarah Evans had her vision some 30 years before Trevithick first introduced steam locomotive power. But the vision became well known locally, and the story was passed down from generation to generation. At last it started to be looked on as a prophecy. When the railway came to Pembrokeshire in the 1850s the residents of the Treffgarne area thought that the prophecy was about to be fulfilled. But Isambard Kingdom Brunel and the other railway engineers were defeated in their attempts to extend the South Wales Railway northwards from Haverfordwest to Fishguard by lack of cash and by the steep gradients and extremely hard rocks in the gorge. Not until the turn of the century did the GWR manage to complete a railway line through Treffgarne Gorge.

On 30th August 1906 a line of carriages with a steaming locomotive in front thundered through the gorge for the first time, precisely as Sarah Evans had foreseen 136 years earlier. Soon there was a regular passenger service, summer and winter. And although diesel engines have now replaced steam locomotives, the carriages have continued to travel very fast through the gorge to this day.

Date : 1770   Sources : Roberts p.22, Worsley p.59, Radford p.152

Soon there was a regular passenger service, summer and winter.

3.18 The Smalls Lighthouse Incident

The Smalls Lighthouse is located on a dangerous reef of rock far out to sea beyond the gannet island of Grassholm. It has been the scene of many shipwrecks, and one of the earliest of the Pembrokeshire lighthouses was built here by Henry Whiteside in 1775-76. It had a revolutionary design, with an octagonal house supported on nine massive legs, six made of huge timbers and the other three of cast iron. The lighthouse stood for 80 years and was in its day the most profitable light in the world; but it is best remembered not for its commercial success but for a gruesome incident which occured in the stormy autumn of 1780.

Two men were on duty at the lighthouse when one of them, Joseph Harry, died suddenly during a violent storn. Since they had not been on the best of terms Thomas Griffiths, his erstwhile companion, became afraid lest he should be suspected of foul play; and so he decided not to cast the corpse into the sea. But as the days passed the corpse began to putrify. Accordingly Tom made a crude wooden box from some of the interior fittings of the house, and placed the body inside. Then he lashed it to the lantern rail so that it should be visible from passing vessels. Various passing ships noticed the strange object, but although poor Tom tried frantically to get them to stop none of them realised that there was anything amiss. Like a good lighthouse keeper, he kept the light working, so passing ships' captains assumed that all was well. And as the storms continued, the box began to fall apart, and a fleshless bony hand tapped against the lantern glass with every fresh assault of the screaming salt-laden wind.....

Tom Griffiths was not relieved on the light until the storms had abated around 25th October, 60 days after the death of his companion. When the relief vessel arrived the poor man was quite mad. The corpse in its box had almost rotted away, and the box itself had been battered to pieces by the storms. The lonely days and nights in the nine-legged tower, lashed by high winds and storm waves, had exacted a terrible price, for Tom Griffiths had been alone with his grisly companion with nothing to divert his mind except the daily routine of tending the light. Joseph Harry was buried in the Whitchurch parish churchyard (Solva) on 28th October, 1780; Thomas Griffiths spent the rest of his days in a lunatic asylum, and died in 1800.

The Smalls Lighthouse Incident taught Trinity House an important lesson, and since 1780 all lighthouses have been manned by three keepers working together and fitted with adequate equipment for sending distress signals.

Date : 1780   *Source : Worsley p.78-9*

3.19 The Red-Haired Steward of Stackpole

In the twelfth century Elidore de Stackpole was one of the knights who was newly established in the colony of Little England Beyond Wales. The affairs of his estate were in the capable hands of a steward, but one day a young red-headed man who called himself Simon appeared on the scene and took over the steward's job with such panache that nobody thought of rebuking him. First he took over the keys to all the rooms in the lord's house, and then he began to manage all the business matters of the house and land with such prudence and providence that everybody was delighted. Whenever his master or mistress secretly thought of some new item of clothing, or some new food, or some item for the house, it would be miraculously procured by the young man, who would simply say "You wished that to be done, and it shall be done for you."

The lord and lady of the manor appeared to have no secrets from Simon, for he knew where all their most treasured possessions were hidden as well as being able to read their thoughts. They tried to economise and to put some of their money aside as insurance against a rainy day, but the young man took to telling them off, saying "Why are you afraid to spend your gold and silver, since your lives are so short and since your savings will never be of any use to you?" Then he began to display distinctly socialist tendencies, serving the choicest meat and drink to the rustics and hired servants and justifying his generosity by saying that those who laboured hardest on the estate should be rewarded with the most abundant supplies.

At last young Simon let his ambition get the better of him, and he took to making decisions about the running of the estate without any reference to his master or mistress. In effect, he took over the whole estate, much to the irritation of everybody except the well-fed rustics. Then it was noticed that he never showed any signs of devotion to God, and he never went to church. Furthermore, nobody knew what happened to him at night, for he never slept in the manor. And yet he was always in his office bright and early every morning, going about his duties.

At last some of the family took to spying on him, and it was discovered that he spent the nights near a mill where there was a pool of water. Furthermore, he could be seen there talking to shadowy unknown persons. This convinced Elidore that something fishy was going on, and he summoned Simon to his room to give him his discharge and to ask for the keys of the estate to be returned. The red-haired steward handed back the keys without question, having held them for more than 40 days. Upon being interrogated by the lord of the manor as to who he was, Simon simply replied enigmatically that "he was begotten upon the wife of a local rustic by a demon who appeared in the form of her husband". And so Simon disappeared from Stackpole as suddenly as he had arrived.

Date : c 1150   Source : Giraldus p.154

3.20 Full Speed in the Fog

The year 1906 saw the launch of a very special ship at the Royal Naval Dockyard at Pembroke Dock. This was the **Montague,** the first ship to be fitted with wireless communications. When she had been fitted out she was reputed to be the most up-to-date vessel in the Navy, and many of the old hands among the work-force expressed their disbelief when told that she could communicate freely with her shore base when she was far away at sea. The wireless operators were not too sure about their magical equipment, either, for it had a tendency to give them rather nasty electric shocks.

At any rate, confidence was high when the **Montague** set out from Pembroke Dock for her high-speed trials. Once out of the Milford Haven waterway, she turned southwards and then south-eastwards into the Bristol Channel, her steam engines going flat out as she built up speed. There was only one problem - fog. Visibility was deteriorating rapidly, but the crackling wireless was working splendidly, and the officers on board were quite sure that all was well as long as they were in touch with the mainland. Some of the grizzled sailors on board saw the enveloping fog as an omen of doom, and complained that it was foolhardy to press on at such speed in such foggy conditions; but the officers took no notice, apart from sending a boy up aloft to the crow's nest to keep a lookout for other vessels.

Soon the ship was making thirty knots, and there was so much noise from the engines and from the crackling wireless on the bridge that nobody heard the boy's faint cries of "Land ahead! Land ahead!" from the crow's nest high above. Nobody, apparently had bothered to consult the charts or to calculate the ship's position, and so nobody apart from the lookout knew that the vessel was heading straight for Lundy Island at full speed. And so, after only six hours at sea, the **Montague** ran straight into Lundy Island, not far from the island's lower light. She was a total loss, and her hulk can still be seen in the deep water beneath the cliffs as a monument to the march of progress.

Date : 1906 *Source : Worsley p.57*

3.21 The Flying Farmer of Eglwyswrw

It was a fine calm moonlit night in winter, and David Thomas of Henllan was walking home along the main road from from Eglwyswrw towards Felindre Farchog. He had been into the village to fetch some medicine for a sick animal from the shop. Suddenly, at about 7 pm (afterwards he remembered the time quite clearly), he found himself in total darkness, being carried through the air back to Eglwyswrw by a *crefishgyn* or spirit. When he felt his feet on the ground again he realised that he was back in the middle of the village, hanging onto the iron bars of the churchyard gate. During his flight he had passed the blacksmith's shop, where several men were at work; but afterwards he ascertained that they had not seen him, nor had he seen them, while being transported through the air.

This is a strange story of transport **towards** the churchyard, for there is a local tradition that St Wrw, the local female saint who was buried in the chantry chapel, was so pure that she "would not have any bedfellows". Consequently she would cast out any male corpse that happened to be interred there. In other words, any flying corpses encountered would be en route **out** of the churchyard rather than towards it. At any rate, David Thomas of Henllan was very frightened by his ordeal, and took it as a sign of his imminent death. However, he is believed to have survived, after his strange flight, to a ripe old age.

Date : c 1850 ? *Source : Davies p.198*

3.22 The Colby Moor Rout

During the early part of the Civil War the sympathies of most Welsh-speaking Pembrokeshire lay with the King, while the Parliamentary cause received much greater support in the South. During 1643 and 1644 there was a complicated ebb and flow in the old county as the Royalist army advanced and then retreated, with the dashing Colonel Rowland Laugharne, for the Parliamentarians, proving to be a constant thorn in its side. During the early part of 1645 it looked as if the Parliamentary cause in Pembrokeshire was finally lost, for Colonel Laugharne suffered a severe defeat at Newcastle Emlyn and then had to retreat as one town after another was lost to the Royalists. At last, by the middle of the Summer, only Pembroke and Tenby were holding out for Parliament, and the Royalist commanders were confident that they could press home their advantage.

It was against this background that the most famous battle to be fought in Pembrokeshire took place, on a bleak moorland half-way between Wiston and Llawhaden. The Royalist commander, Colonel Gerrard, had to leave his campaigns in West Wales to help the King elsewhere, and this provided the opportunity which Colonel Laugharne had been waiting for. In any case, Gerrard had made himself most unpopular in Pembrokeshire because of the heavy demands he made on local people for the maintenance

...only Pembroke and Tenby were holding out for Parliament, and the Royalist commanders were confident that they could press home their advantage.

of his army; and his troops gained a reputation for firing crops, burning down farm buildings, plundering houses and farms, and even murdering innocent civilians. On the command of the King, Gerrard left Haverfordwest in July 1645 with 2,000 foot-soldiers and 700 cavalrymen, never to return.

Towards the end of July Colonel Laugharne decided that the time was ripe for the recovery of Pembrokeshire for Parliament; news had reached him of Gerrard's return to England, and there were rumours that the Royalist garrison at Haverfordwest was planning to burn many of the local cornfields, which were ripening well in the hot summer weather. On 29th July Laugharne moved out of Pembroke with 500 infantrymen and 200 horsemen, accompanied by two small guns. He was joined by 250 seamen landed from the Parliamentary vessel **Warwick** just downstream from Blackpool on the Eastern Cleddau. These forces combined not far from Canaston Bridge. The Royalist commanders, Stradling and Egerton, were unaware of the enemy strength since a party of six of their scouts had been captured by Laugharne's soldiers before they could send a message back to the Haverfordwest garrison.

On Friday 1st August a Royalist force of about 1,500 men, including 450 on horseback, left Haverfordwest and headed towards Narberth. About 6 o'clock in the evening they were engaged in a battle by the Parliamentarians. At first Laugharne deployed only 150 musketeers and a small number of cavalry. For about one hour the fighting was fierce and indecisive, but then Laugharne sent in the rest of his cavalry. His horsemen first routed the Royalist cavalry, and while some of them pursued the enemy back towards Haverfordwest the rest of them fell upon the Royalist foot-soldiers with deadly effect. Soon the battle was over, leaving 150 Royalists dead and 700 taken prisoner. Among the dead were five members of the Foley family of Ridgeway, Llawhaden. Virtually all the Royalist arms, carriages and provisions were also seized. On the Parliamentarian side, only two men were killed, and this incredible disparity in losses led to local speculation that the hand of God must have played a part in the battle. In any case the "Colby Moor Rout" entered into local mythology, and to this day the expression is used in conversation by Pembrokeshire people when they are describing a scene of utter confusion.

Although the Colby Moor Rout was more of a local skirmish than a battle in the grand style, its strategic importance was great. Laugharne went on to take Haverfordwest, while most of the Cavaliers who had avoided capture at Colby Moor fled to Carmarthen. The Parliamentarians never lost their momentum, and after taking Carew, Manorbier and Picton Castles the whole of Pembrokeshire came under Laugharne's control. By Christmas the whole of South Wales was won, and Laugharne was the hero of the hour. The First Civil War was at an end.

There is one gruesome footnote to the Colby Moor Rout. When, in 1864, restoration work was under way in Slebech Parish Church, about one mile from the battle site, piles of human bones were discovered beneath the pews. They were taken away by the cartload, and it can only be assumed that they were the bones of the unfortunate Royalist soldiers who died at Colby Moor.

Date : 1645   *Source : Leach p.110*

3.23 Rebecca and Her Hosts

In the period 1830-1850 there was a severe farming depression in West Wales, with low prices for farm products, high rents, too many small farmers, and too many mouths to feed in the countryside. The large landowners were enclosing more and more land, and many small turnpike trusts came into being which were improving roads and charging tolls on those who used them. Some of the turnpike trusts erected new toll-gates at frequent intervals even though their roads were in a poor state of repair, and farmers were often charged tolls for carting lime or moving cattle from one part of a farm to another. Great resentment built up, and on the night of 13th May 1839 things came to a head with the destruction of a toll-gate at Efailwen, with the toll-collector's house set ablaze.

This was the signal for an outbreak of toll-gate destruction all over West Wales which lasted for almost 5 years. The Efailwen gate was re-erected and protected by seven special constables, but on the night of 6th June a mob of about 400 arrived on the scene, drove off the constables and smashed down the gate and the toll-house. All were disguised; some wore women's clothes and had blackened faces. A week or so later another mob, similarly disguised, smashed down a gate near Whitland. Then on 17th July, the Efailwen gate was smashed down for the third time by a crowd of "black-faced women" with a leader referred to as "Becca". This was a remarkable victory, for this time the Efailwen gate was not rebuilt, and in response to the unrest a further four gates were dismantled in the Whitland area. So was born the legend of Rebecca and her daughters.

Where did the name Rebecca come from? We should remember that the poor tenant farmers of the early nineteenth century were familiar with only one book - the Bible. And the nonconformist churches of the day placed greater stress on the harsh theology of the Old Testament than on the theology of love enshrined in the New. So the zealous chapelgoers who took part in the first toll-gate riots were quite familiar with the verse from the Book of Genesis: "And they blessed Rebecca and said unto her, thou art our sister; be thou the mother of thousands of millions, and let thy seed possess the gate of those who hate them". We do not know who first decided that this verse should be the motto of the rioters, but it may well have been a pugilist and small-holder from Mynachlogddu who was known as Twm Carnabwth. He may well have been the original Rebecca, but the authorities were never able to prove it.

In 1842-3 the rioting got worse, with toll-gates destroyed in St Clears, Haverfordwest, Narberth, Robeston Wathen, Scleddau and in many other places. Hundreds of people took part in the riots, but always the rioters were led by Rebecca and her black-faced daughters. There was no shortage of men inclined to play the role of Rebecca, and no shortage of followers. Before long gates were being destroyed in Carmarthenshire and Cardiganshire, and further afield in South Wales. Local militiamen, professional troops and special constables were pressed into service to quell the riots, and the Government became seriously concerned about the possible breakdown of law and order. Rebecca and her daughters became adept at evading the forces of the law, and greater secrecy and stealth became necessary.

Unfortunately the hosts of Rebecca eventually acquired a lunatic fringe, with a gang led by Shoni Sgubor Fawr and Dai'r Cantwr terrorising the countryside west of Llanelli. There were a number of injuries and deaths; spies and informers were enlisted on both sides; shadowy figures moved about at night, and strange coaches were seen rushing along the country lanes. Some of the rioters were captured, tried and deported.

But the riots were ultimately successful. A Parliamentary Commission which met in 1844 resulted in legislation which removed most of the grievances of the small farmers, and the Rebecca Riots ended as quickly as they had begun.

Date : 1839-44   *Sources : D. Williams, Molloy*

3.24 A Circumstance at Haverford Castle

During the time of the Earl of Clare a "famous circumstance" happened in the fortress at Haverfordwest. The castle was built around 1138, but it looked very different from the battered stone fortress of today. There may have been a stone keep at the time, but probably the towers and main defensive walls were made of wood.

Around 1150 a famous robber was chained up in a dungeon beneath one of the towers of the castle. There was little chance of him escaping, so security was somewhat lax. Three of the lads who lived within the castle walls made a habit of visiting the prisoner; one of them was the son of Gilbert de Clare, another was the son of the castle tenant, who may have been Richard Fitz Tancred, and the third was the tenant's grandson. All three were at the castle in order to receive a good education. In their spare time they visited the fettered prisoner in the dungeon, who used to teach them to make arrows.

One day the boys asked if the robber could be brought up from the dungeon to help them make some more arrows. The gaoler agreed, and brought him up to the tower, but when his back was turned the robber slammed the door of the tower room and barricaded himself inside with the boys. Immediately a great clamour went up, with the gaoler and everybody else outside trying to batter down the door, and the boys screaming and crying inside the room. The robber grabbed the axe that was used for splitting and shaping arrows and threatened the lives of the boys with such ferocity that he found himself in an unassailable negotiating position.

In due course, the robber secured the promise of "indemnity and security" in the most ample manner, and at last he released the boys and allowed their frantic parents into the tower room. The lord of the castle was true to his word, and the robber was released from his chains and allowed to go free.

Date : c 1150   *Source : Giraldus p.142*

3.25 Three Brothers of Moylgrove

There were three brothers called Wil, Siôn and Dai, who jointly owned and worked a farm near the coast. Let us say that it was not far from Moylgrove. One day, Wil, the youngest, was out ploughing with a pair of oxen, when one of them died. Sadly Wil took the other ox home and told his brothers what had happened. They would not believe him, and they were so furious that they determined to murder him. They bound him with ropes, put him in a sack, and threw him into the sea over the cliffs at Ceibwr. They believed him to be dead, but somehow Wil managed to struggle free and swim ashore. Unknown to his brothers, he skinned the dead ox, disposed of the carcass and went away.

In due course he came to Cardigan, where he sold the hide. Now he had a little money in his pocket, but he had to sleep rough, and he was at a loss how to earn a living. One day he found a wounded bird, which he tended until it was well. Then he had an idea. He hid his money here and there outside the town and then went in to the market-place. As his clothes were very ragged and as he carried the bird with great care, people took him for an idiot and started to question him.

"Where art thou taking the bird?" asked one.
"Along with me", answered Wil.
"What dost thou do with it?"
"I shall not tell thee."

Many a question they asked him, getting only the same replies, until they were quite convinced that he was soft in the head. Then he told one of the townsfolk that the bird was a very special one which could find treasure. This news immediately spread all around the market-place. Someone asked the price of the bird. Wil said it was not for sale.

"I'll give thee a pound for it", said one.
"I can find a pound a day with this bird", said Wil.
"Thou art a liar!"
"Very well, believe me or not, I don't care which."

By this time a good crowd had gathered, and at last Wil agreed to put the bird to the test. Heading out of town, Wil led the crowd towards the places where he had hidden his savings. Before getting there he stopped and placed the bird near the hedge, saying it would cry out if there was treasure anywhere near. The bird remained silent. The test was repeated a little further on, and still the bird did not cry. By now he was being ridiculed by the crowd, but then he came to one of the spots where he had hidden his money. Wil squeezed the bird, causing it to cry out. Then, digging into the undergrowth, he took out the money. He repeated this several times, making his audience more and more excited. Now everybody wanted to buy the bird. First Wil refused to name his price, but at last he sold it to an old Cardi miser for a hundred pounds.

Wil went on his way and came at last to Eglwyswrw, where he bought a drove of sheep with all his money. Then he returned home. On seeing him Siôn and Dai were frightened out of their wits, believing him to be a ghost. At last they overcame their fear and began to question him.

"Where didst thou get the sheep? asked Dai.
"At the bottom of the sea", said Wil, "and had I anyone to help me, I should have had more - it's hard to catch them down there."

"Where are they then?"

"O, just as they are up here, grazing where the grass is best, and that is always in the valleys where the water is deepest. If you like, I'll show you where the best places are."

So the three brothers went down to the edge of the cliff at Ceibwr. Standing close to the edge, above the deep water, Wil pointed into the depths. Siôn, being the decisive one, leaped in at once, and Wil and Dai heard the gurgle in his throat as he sank out of sight.

"What is that noise?" asked Dai.

"He is laughing and taking the best sheep! Quick - follow him at once!" cried Wil.

Dai took the leap into the sea. Wil took the whole farm.

Date : c 1750   Source : T.G. Jones, p.225

3.26 The Boy in the Bell

During the Civil War many atrocities were committed in Pembrokeshire by both the Royalists and the Parliamentarians, but one of the events which created a sense of outrage in the county for many generations afterwards was the sacking of St David's Cathedral in 1648 by Parliamentary soldiers.

Tom Williams was ten years old at the time. He lived near the Cathedral and spent much of his time playing there. He knew all of the buildings inside out, and one day when the Parliamentary soldiers arrived in order to do their dastardly work, Tom happened to be playing on one of the high galleries overlooking the nave. He watched, appalled, while they smashed the stained-glass windows, removed many of the fine church ornaments, and started to pull down the organ. The men had all taken off their helmets and heavy protective clothing for the work, since it was a hot summer's day. In his fury at the sacrilege, Tom threw down a large piece of rubble at the soldiers, hitting one of them on the head. Blood flowed freely from the soldier's wound. Unfortunately for Tom, one of the soldiers had spotted him on the high gallery, and a number of them immediately started to climb the steps in order to catch him. Tom was almost paralysed with fear for he was totally cut off. He had no option but to climb high into the bell tower as he heard the heavy footsteps behind him coming ever closer. He thought that all was lost, but being a bright lad, he suddenly realised that one of the bells was large enough to hide him. Quickly he climbed inside and hung there on the clapper, hardly daring to breathe. The soldiers rushed into the bell tower, searched everywhere, and then left again, furious that the boy had eluded them.

Later on, under cover of darkness, when all was quiet in the Cathedral, Tom descended from the bell tower and slipped quietly through the tombstones, afraid that the heavy beating of his heart should be heard by the Parliamentary soldiers who were camped nearby. His was indeed a lucky escape, for a few days later the very bell inside which he had hidden was removed by the soldiers, while they also stripped most of the lead from the Cathedral roof.

Date : 1648   Source : Fenton p.47

3.27 The Golden Idol of Trewern

Trewern is an ancient manor house not far from Nevern and about a mile from the cromlech of Pentre Ifan. It was owned by the Warren family, said to have been descended from Gwynfardd, the prince who ruled Cemais at the time of the Norman Invasion. In the eighteenth century, and for as long as anybody could remember, the house had been haunted. Strange noises were often heard in the rooms, dishes would dance about in the kitchen of their own accord, and sometimes a lady dressed in a long silk dress would be seen. There appeared to be more than one ghost in the house, and although many attempts were made at exorcism the hauntings continued. The house was struck with misfortune, and in 1787 there was no male heir to the Trewern estate for the first time in 700 years. The last of the Warren family, old Edward Warren Jones, died a batchelor at Trewern in 1829, and the mansion fell into other hands. Finally, things became so bad that nobody wanted to live at Trewern, and it appeared that the house would soon be abandoned to its fate.

But then, around the year 1830, the fortunes of the old house were transformed. The sole occupants of the house were a tenant farmer and two old servants, surviving as best they could with few of the luxuries of life. But then the farmer suddenly acquired fine clothes and new furnishings. The old house was repaired and tidied up; new farm animals were purchased at Cardigan mart; and the servants were seen in Newport buying food, wine and other household items on a lavish scale. New farm buildings were built, and the land was improved through better husbandry and improved crops. All of this needed money, but try as they might the neighbours could not discover where the money was coming from. For several years Trewern continued to rise in the estimation of the neighbours, but still none of them could work out the reason for the tenant farmer's new-found wealth. The mystery deepened when it was noticed that he regularly left Trewern in his coach and stayed away for several weeks; and that whenever he returned there would be more lavish expenditure.

At last the farmer died and the secret leaked out. It was revealed by an old servant that one of the resident ghosts of Trewern had told the farmer of an "image of great value" sealed inside the wall of an upstairs room, immediately above the main entrance. A search was made, and sure enough a large pagan idol, made of solid gold, was found in a hidden recess. The farmer swore his servants to secrecy, and started to turn the image into money. Every now and then he would knock off a piece of the image and set off with it to London, where he would sell it at the best possible price before returning with hard cash. In this way, over the years, he sold the whole image, and nobody was the wiser. After the image was found and disposed of, the ghosts of Trewern disappeared, and there were no more noises at night nor broken dishes.

So the good times returned to Trewern, and it was said locally that the tenant farmer left £50,000 in his will to a son who lived outside the local area. It was also rumoured among the neighbours that the pagan image had been stolen hundreds of years earlier from an ancient Druid site among the oak groves of Pentre Ifan or Tycanol.

Date : c 1840   *Source : Evans Wentz p.156*

3.28 The Sad Loss of the "Roebuck"

One of the least successful firefighting episodes in Pembrokeshire history occurred at Neyland on a January night in 1905. The GWR passenger ferry **Roebuck,** one of the company's best ships, was tied up alongside the Neyland fish quay. She was a fine vessel, capable of steaming at 20 knots and providing accommodation for 850 passengers. It was a bitterly cold night, with sub-zero temperatures and sheets of ice on land and on the decks and superstructure of the ship. The steward of the vessel, a Mr Harwood, had left the vessel at 7.30 pm and was returning on board around midnight. As he climbed the gangplank he heard the fire alarm go off, and it was soon apparent that there was a serious fire on board.

The GWR fire brigade, based at the Neyland rail depot, was quickly on the scene. The firefighting team had only very recently been formed, and never before had they fought a fire. In no time at all 140 firemen had turned out, and for three hours they fought the blaze with commendable enthusiasm. The flames from the burning vessel were visible for miles around, and a large crowd assembled at the fish quay to watch the heroic efforts of the firefighters. So enthusiastic were they with their powerful pumps and hoses that they all but filled the vessel with water. The tide at this time was low; and unknown to the firemen, the ship was sitting on the bottom. Furthermore, nobody appeared to notice that the blaze had caused many of the porthole windows to shatter.

But now the firemen were really getting into their stride, and they continued to deluge the ship with water. Then the tide began to rise. Since the **Roebuck** had now lost all her buoyancy, sea water began to flood in through the broken portholes into the engine room, and before long it was flowing over the decks and down the stairways and hatches as well. By the following morning, nine hours after the alarm was raised, the ship was almost submerged by the high tide, with only its masts and funnels visible above the surface. No doubt delighted that they had managed to put the fire out, the GWR firemen all went off home for a well-earned rest, with the cheers of the onlookers ringing in their ears.

Date : 1905   *Source : Pembs Mag 26*

PEMBROKESHIRE FOLK TALES

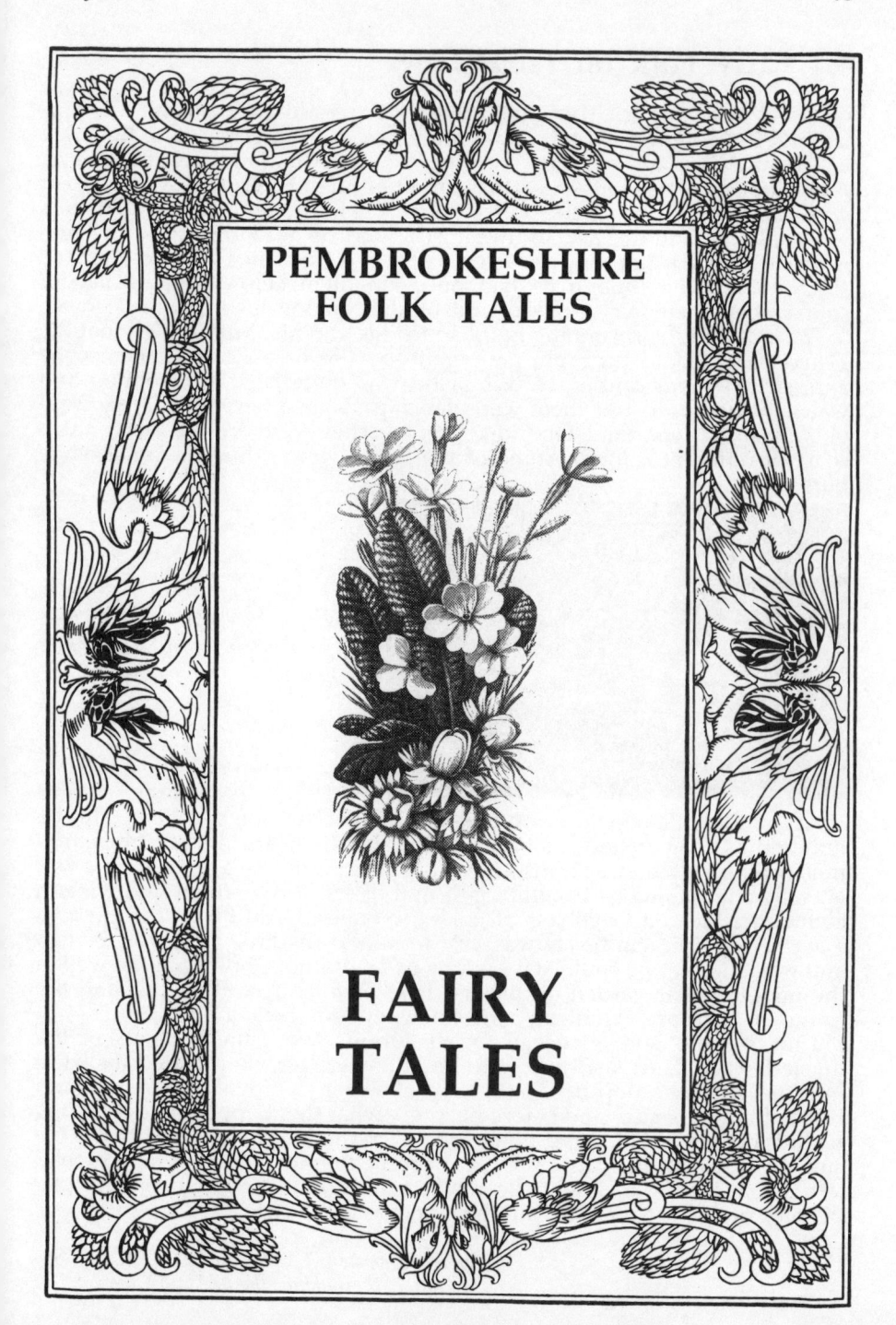

FAIRY TALES

4.1 Fairy Folk on Freni Fawr

Once upon a time a lad of about twelve years old was looking after his father's sheep on Freni Fach, a hill not far from Crymych. A fine June day was in prospect, and the early morning mist was draining from the valleys. As he looked across to the nearby summit of Freni Fawr he saw a group of small figures moving about on the hillside. He thought at first that they were soliders. He decided to investigate, and on walking across to Freni Fawr he realised that they were the *Tylwyth Teg* or Fair Folk. He knew all about them even though he had not seen them before, but he had of course seen their fairy rings of mushrooms in the lush summer grass.

The lad thought of running home to tell his parents, but decided that the *Tylwyth Teg* would probably have gone by the time he returned; so he approached them cautiously. When he was quite close he stopped and watched them. Most of them were dancing inside a fairy ring. They were of both sexes, very handsome and cheerful. They were dressed elegantly in coats of different colours. Some of the ladies were riding on small white horses.

When he was quite close he stopped and watched them.

At last the little people saw him and motioned for him to join in. This he did, and as soon as he set foot inside the ring he heard the most beautiful music. Suddenly he was transported to a magnificent palace, where he was liberally entertained by beautiful girls and offered exotic foods and wine in abundance, served in goblets of gold. He realised that he was in *Gwlad y Tylwyth Teg* (Fairyland). He was able to talk to the little people in Welsh, and was told that he could stay so long as he did not drink from the well in the middle of the garden of flowers. He solemnly agreed to this, and the round of pleasures went on - he knew not for how long.

Time passed, and he began to get curious about the contents of the mysterious well. At last, unable to resist any longer, he plunged his hand into the well to scoop up a mouthful of water. Suddenly pandemonium reigned in the palace, and before he knew what was happening everything had disappeared. He found himself back on the hillside of Freni Fawr; the sun was high and he could see his sheep peacefully grazing where he had left them. Try as he might, he never again found any sign of the little people, or their fairy ring, or their enchanted palace.

Date : 1700s ?   Sources : Roberts p.13, Radford p.92, Sikes p.84,
                                Howells 1831, Davies p,105

4.2 Gruffydd and the Invisible Islands

Long ago there were green fertile islands out at sea beyond the Pembrokeshire coast, populated by the Fairy Folk *(Plant Rhys Ddwfn* in Welsh). The strange thing about these islands was that sometimes they could be seen and sometimes not, even when the weather was clear and the sunlight bright. Once upon a time Gruffydd ab Einon was told about the islands; day after day he stared out to sea, sometimes climbing up a tall tree to get a better view. However, one day he was standing in St David's churchyard when he saw the green islands out to sea. He ran down to the shore and put to sea in his boat but found that the islands had disappeared. The same thing happened a second time, but on the third occasion he took with him the piece of turf on which he had been standing in the churchyard, and the islands remained in view. This time he landed safely, to be welcomed by the fairy folk and to be shown their many wonderful treasures. On enquiring, Gruffydd was told that there were strange herbs on the islands which rendered them invisible, and that these herbs grew elsewhere only in St David's churchyard and on one square yard of turf somewhere in the old hundred of Cemais. Only by standing on the right place and by carrying a piece of the special turf with one is it possible to find the islands and set foot on them. Apparently Gruffydd continued to visit the islands for many years, becoming a good friend of the fairy folk and becoming very wealthy into the bargain. Undoubtedly, the islands are still there, visible only to those who stand on the right spot.....

Date : c 1650 ?
Sources : Radford p.95, Davies p.91, Roberts p.7, Parry-Jones p.21

.....day after day he stared out to sea, sometimes climbing up a tall tree to get a better view.

4.3 The Tempting of Crythor

Many, many years ago a young man with golden hair and blue eyes hired a cottage not far from Amroth. He was named Crythor, after the old Welsh stringed instrument, the *crwth,* which he played brilliantly; and whenever a *Noson Lawen* was being held in the villages round about he would play on his fiddle until the people were too weary to dance any longer.

One summer evening when the merry-making was over he was returning to his cottage among the gentle green hills when he came across a band of fairy folk *(Tylwyth Teg)* dressed in scarlet and green. They were standing in a wooded glade, and they were quite unafraid as he approached. "Crythor", said one with a mischievous grin, "make music for us so that we can dance". So Crythor, being an amiable sort of fellow, played his fiddle while they leapt and tripped and weaved about him in the moonlight.

At last, as the dawn approached, the little people began to drift away, but before the last fairy disappeared into the shadows she turned to Crythor and said "Remember, my friend, that under the hills not far away there is a cave that goes on for ever. Inside it, your fiddle will turn to gold and you will learn the music of the Fair Folk."

This was an offer too good to resist, for Crythor had always been poor, and the magical haunting melodies of the *Tylwyth Teg* were the wonder of country folk everywhere. Just think how famous he would be if he could play fairy music on a golden fiddle! So he started to search for the cave. He asked everyone and hunted everywhere, and kept on searching as summer turned to autumn and as autumn turned to winter. By now the quest for the cave was an obsession. Every time he found a cave he would enter it and call into the darkness "Is anyone there?" Then he would play the tunes he had played to the little people in the fairy dell all those months before. He never received an answer to his question, and nobody ever appeared to dance to his tunes.

Then, one day in the depths of winter when the snow was lying in deep drifts across the lifeless landscape, he set off into the hills again to find his magic cave. He was never seen again. Some folks say he found his cave. Others say he was lost in the snowdrifts. But some of the old people of the district say that if you take the footpath through the hills north of Pendine you can hear strange music echoing in a deep underground cavern, where the ghost of Crythor plays the music of the *Tylwyth Teg* on a ghostly golden fiddle.

. . . he would play on his fiddle until the people were too weary to dance any longer.

Date : c 1750 ?   Source : Radford p.115

4.4 Elidorus and the Fair Folk

Elidorus (Elidyr) was a priest who told this story from his childhood to David II, who was Bishop of St Davids around 1150. Apparently, when Elidorus was twelve years old (a good age for encountering fairies) he was living not far from a deep river valley. He hated school, and one day he ran away in order to escape from the strict discipline and frequent beatings. He hid in a river bank where he found a convenient hollow, and stayed there for two days and nights. At last, just as he was at his lowest ebb, feeling both hungry and miserable, two little men appeared. They invited him to join them in a land "full of delights and sports". He followed them willingly and after walking along a dark path they came out at last into a beautiful countryside of woods and fields, with meadows full of flowers and rivers and springs of crystal-clear water.

Elidorus was taken to see the King, who questioned him at length before giving him into the care of his son, who was about his own age. They played together, and the King's son taught Elidorus the special language of the *Tylwyth Teg* or Fair Folk. After that he passed freely back and forth between the fairy world and his own, sometimes following the same dark path and sometimes by different routes.

He described the little people to his mother, saying that they were small but well-built, with long hair and fair complexions. They had small greyhounds and horses; they lived largely on a milk diet but ate no meat or fish; they never swore nor told lies; they had no form of public worship but were devoted to openness and truth; and they were constantly amazed by the many vices of the human folk whom they met when they attended the weekly markets in the nearby towns.

Elidorus told his mother that when he was with the King's son they often played with balls made of pure gold. At first she was simply intrigued; but then, since she was desperately poor she became greedy and insisted that her son should steal a golden ball for her on his next visit. Reluctantly, and with a great sense of guilt, Elidorus took one of the balls and, hoping that none of his friends had noticed, rushed home with it. But then he noticed that he was being followed by two little men, and just before he reached the cottage door he stumbled and fell. He dropped the golden ball, and in a flash the little men had seized it. They scolded him roundly for his inconstancy and treachery, and ran back towards *Gwlad y Tylwyth Teg*, their enchanted kingdom. Tearfully Elidorus tried to explain, and he ran after them towards the magic passage on the river bank. But search as he would, he failed to find it even though he had passed that way many times. And nor did he ever find it again.....

Elidorus took a long time to get over his sense of desolation at the loss of his friends, but recover he did, and he went on to become a famous priest in the diocese of St David's.

Date : c 1110 ?   Sources : Roberts p.8, Giraldus p.133, G. Jones, p.164, Thomas p.42

4.5 The Old Man of Llech-y-Derwydd

Llech-y-Derwydd (or Llech-y-Deri) was a big farm in north Pembrokeshire where there was enough work for the farmer and his family and also for various servant boys and girls. Owain, who was the son and heir of the farm and Elfed, the head servant boy, were inseparable friends, and the latter was treated just like a brother in the close-knit family. When Owain was given new clothes, so was Elfed; when the son was taken to market or given some special treat, so was his friend.

In due course the two got married to two young women of the neighbourhood, and Elfed and his new wife settled in a cottage on the farm, where he continued to work. One day, about six months after Owain had married, the two friends went out for a day's shooting around the rocky tor of Carn Alw, and they temporarily lost sight of one another. Coming round the flank of the rock, Elfed thought he heard the sound of sweet music. He whistled and shouted for his friend, but there was no reply. He searched through the great crags and boulders, but there was no sign of him. Owain had disappeared without trace. He hunted high and low for the rest of the day, returning to the farm only at dusk to tell the distraught family that their son had disappeared. Nor did he return that night. Next morning family, friends and neighbours set off for the mountain, and a thorough search was made from the spot where the two had separated.

Owain's young wife was distraught, waiting in vain for him to return as she watched the hills from her window day after day.

They found no trace of Owain, but when they found a fairy ring near the spot where he had last been seen they feared the worst. When Elfed told how he had heard the faint sounds of music at about the time his friend vanished, they all knew that he had stepped into a fairy ring while the fairies were dancing there, and had been transported away to their enchanted kingdom.

Owain's young wife was distraught, waiting in vain for him to return as she watched the hills from her window day after day. Weeks and months passed. At last she gave birth to a child who was named Dewi. As the years rolled by the child grew up to be a man, and eventually he married also. Owain was almost forgotten, but Dewi remembered the story of the disappearance of his father, and in due course told the story to his sons when they were old enough to understand. More years rolled by; Owain's parents both died, and so did his wife. Memories faded, and Llech-y-Derwydd was occupied by Dewi and his family.

One day, during a windy and boisterous October, when Dewi was away at Cardigan market, a tall, thin old man with a white beard appeared, shuffling along the lane to the farmhouse. Dewi's wife was not particularly kind or sympathetic, and believing the old man to be a drunken old vagabond she shouted to him to go away. He paid no attention, but calmly came up to the front door, opened it and walked inside. Then he asked for his parents. Dewi's wife became angry and accused him of being drunk; but she was taken aback when he claimed that he had gone out hunting only the day before, and then apologised for staying out all night and worrying his wife and parents. He seemed genuinely surprised at the sight of the children and at the changes in the house.

The young mistress explained to him that her father-in-law had been lost for years, and that the neighbours believed him to have been murdered by the old farm servant who lived in the cottage down the lane. This roused the old man, and he declared that this was a lie. Furthermore, he said, the house was his, and he would have his rights. She replied that **she** now lived in the house with Dewi and the children, since the old grandparents and Dewi's mother were long since dead. But then the old man tired of arguing with Dewi's wife, who had become quite angry since he showed no sign of leaving.

Suddenly the old man got up and went outside, and after pottering around the farm for a while he shuffled off down the lane towards the servant's cottage. There he knocked on the door, and on entering found Elfed sitting by the fire. He looked old and infirm, but his face lit up as he recognized his old friend, and as they talked they came to realise that no less than fifty years had passed since that fateful day when they had both gone out for a day's sport. The conversation ranged far and wide and the two old men exchanged many reminiscences about the days of their youth.

As the light began to fade Elfed prevailed upon his visitor to stay and have something to eat. He agreed, but as soon as he touched the food he tumbled to the floor and died. He was later buried by the side of his parents and his wife in the local churchyard. But because of the rudeness of the young mistress of Llech-y-Derwydd a curse fell upon the house, which remained for many generations until it had been sold nine times.

Date : c 1800 ?   Sources : Parry-Jones p.31, Davies p.114, Rhys p.152

4.6 Einon and his Fairy Bride

This story comes from the Presely Hills, and it was told by old people in the area around Pentre Ifan in the latter part of the last century.

Einon was a shepherd lad who used to take his sheep across the great moor to graze on the northern flank of Mynydd Presely. One day, in cloudy and misty weather, he got lost and wandered about for hours on the moor. At last he came to a hollow place surrounded by rushes, where he saw a number of fairy rings. He knew of the danger of these rings, for other shepherds had warned him about them; but try as he might, he could not walk away from then. Then a little old man appeared, and walked off into the mist. He was merry and blue-eyed, and looked harmless enough, so the boy followed, thinking that he might show him the path off the moor; and he was about to ask for help when the old man suddenly said "Sssh. Do not speak a word till I tell you to!" So Einon kept quiet and followed.

In a little while they came to a tall standing stone. The old man tapped it three times, and then tilted it over. A narrow path with steps descending was revealed, and from it emerged a bluish-white light. "Follow me", said the little old man, "and no harm will come to you." So down they went, the old man in front and Einon behind. Soon the lad was amazed to see a fine wooded country with a beautiful palace, and rivers and mountains. Bird-song filled the air, and as they approached the palace enchanting music echoed between the marble pillars. They entered the palace and feasted on the most wonderful food - but Einon saw no people, and the dishes appeared and later disappeared of their own accord. Now he could hear voices all around him. At last the old man said he could speak, but as he tried to do so he found that he could not move his tongue. This was very puzzling.

But Einon forgot about his minor problem when he saw a smiling old lady coming towards him with three beautiful girls. They were small in stature, but strong and graceful, with fair hair and blue eyes. He had never seen maidens more beautiful than these. The girls spoke to him, but still he could not reply. Then, much to his surprise, one of the girls bent down and kissed him; and all at once he began to converse in their own language fluently and wittily.

Einon stayed in this enchanted land for a year and a day, living with the three fair maidens in the palace and gradually falling in love with one of them whose name was Olwen (for it was she who had first kissed him). Einon thought that no more than a day had passed, for time had no meaning in the land of these beautiful and kind people.

But at last Einon felt a longing to see his family and acquaintances, and thanking the little old man for his kindness he asked if he could return home. The old King (for this is what he was) said "Wait a little while longer", so Einon did as he was told. But at last he determined to go. Olwen begged him not to leave, but when he had made a solemn vow to return on the first day of the new moon she let him go, loaded with treasures.

When Einon arrived home not one of his family or friends recognized him. Everybody believed that he had been murdered by another shepherd, and this poor man had become so afraid of the vengeance of the family

> *People began to ask about Olwen's pedigree, for there was nobody as beautiful as she in the whole of Cemais.*

that he had fled to America. Einon was saddened by this news, but he took care not to say where he had been. In any case there were great celebrations at his return home, and great was the amazement among the neighbours at his new-found wealth.

Then the time of the new moon arrived. Einon remembered his pledge and longed to see Olwen again, so he returned to the other country. There was great rejoicing in the beautiful palace, and before long Einon and Olwen decided that they wanted to marry. And so they became man and wife, but with no great ceremony, for the little people disliked celebration and noise. When the marriage was over, Einon wished to take his beautiful bride back with him to the upper world, and the old King and his people agreed to let them go. They were given two snow-white ponies, and off they went, taking with them as much gold and silver as they could carry.

They reached the upper world safely, and Einon no longer had to earn his meagre living as a shepherd boy. He was able to buy a large estate, and he and his wife lived there most handsomely. There seemed to be no limit to their wealth, or to their generosity with their neighbours, friends and relatives. At last a son was born to them, and he was named Taliesin. He was as fair and beautiful as his mother. People began to ask about Olwen's pedigree, for there was nobody as beautiful as she in the whole of Cemais. Einon never told anybody where Olwen had come from, but at last the whole district took it for granted that she was one of the fairy people.

Einon did not disagree with these rumours, and would say only that Olwen was indeed very fair, and that she had two sisters just as fair as she was. So it was that Einon, Olwen and Taliesin lived happily ever after, with the neighbours all quite convinced that Olwen had come from the land of the Fair Folk or *Tylwyth Teg*. And that is how the little people from the Otherworld first came to be called the Fair Folk.

Date : 1800 or earlier?   Source : Evans Wentz p.161

4.7 Peregrin and the Mermaid

Peregrin was one of the fishermen of St Dogmael's on the Teifi estuary in the early part of the eighteenth century. It was a sunny September afternoon as he pulled his inshore fishing-boat away from the slipway and headed out past Poppit Sands and around the cliffs of Cemais Head. There was good fishing to be had near the cliffs, and since the sea was calm and the tide was high he came in close enough to touch the steep rock face with his oars.

He was out of sight of the rest of the boats in the fishing fleet, around a bend in the cliff face, when he suddenly saw a mermaid sitting in a narrow cleft in the rocks. She did not see Peregrin, for like all the best mermaids she was quite preoccupied with combing her long golden hair and looking at her own reflection in the mirror of the sea surface. A rare pretty piece

Further out beyond the headland, the other fishermen continued quietly to pay out their nets.

she was, and Peregrin, who was never backward with the girls, grabbed her and pulled her aboard in a flash. He thought of having a bit of fun with her, but he was put out of his stride when she began pleading with him piteously, in perfect Welsh.

"Let me go! Let me go!" she wailed. "If you keep me, Peregrin, no good will come out of it; but if you let me go I will save you from the doom that hangs over you."

"What doom is that?" asked Peregrin, intrigued. The mermaid did not reply to the question, but then she said "Let me go, and I'll give you three shouts when you need me most."

Peregrin was in two minds about this, since she was very beautiful, with nothing but her long golden hair to cover her top half. But while he pondered, the mermaid flipped her long fishy tail, slipped out of his grasp and was over the side in an instant. And before he could react she was gone, leaving but a silver gleam in the deep green water beneath the boat.

After his evening's fishing Peregrin returned to the shore, determined never to say a thing about the mermaid to the other fishermen lest he should be laughed at. Day after day went by, with calm seas, good weather and fine fishing. Peregrin saw no sign of the doom which the mermaid had warned him of, but he did not forget, and kept his wits about him just in case.

Then one day, on the calmest and stillest day of the autumn, twenty St Dogmael's men put out to sea to fish the waters beyond Cemais Head. Peregrin was with them, accompanied this time in his boat by a friend who would help with the nets. Flat as a table was the sea, and the line of the horizon out towards Ireland was as sharp as crystal. The sky was as blue and clear as Peregrin had ever seen it. The fishing was good, and the nets were overboard. All of a sudden, not three fathoms from the edge of the boat, there was a silver flash and a flurry on the surface of the sea. Up popped a head of long golden hair. Peregrin immediately recognized the pretty face of the mermaid.

"Peregrin! Peregrin! Peregrin!" she shouted urgently. "Take in your nets! Take in your nets! Take in your nets!" And then she was gone, before Peregrin could ask her why. But he remembered about her warning of doom, and though there was no sign of impending catastrophe he leaped into action. "Get the nets in while I set the oars!" he shouted to his colleague, who was gaping thunderstruck at what he had just witnessed. The two men worked furiously, and within minutes they were rowing for the shore as fast as they could go. Further out beyond the headland, the other fishermen continued quietly to pay out their nets.

Just as Peregrin and his friend reached the lee side of Cemaes Head the storm broke. Nobody could remember its like, for the sky darkened in an instant, with winds that screamed from the west and waves that sent spray flying straight over the high clifftops. There was no hope, in a storm like that, for any small vessels caught out in the open sea, and eighteen St Dogmael's fishermen were lost. But Peregrin and his friend managed to reach the shore at Poppit Sands. Soon they were safe and snug in the local inn, shocked by their narrow escape and mourning the loss of their friends but nonetheless drinking a quiet toast to the mermaid of Cemais Head.

Date : c 1710   Sources: Davies p.144, Styles p.38, Parry-Jones p.84, Rhys p.163

4.8 Ianto and the Lucky Shilling

In the early part of the last century Ianto Llewellyn lived in the countryside not far from Boncath. He used to keep his fire of culm balls burning all night long, just in case the *Tylwyth Teg* should be cold. He was well aware that they came into his kitchen every night, for he often heard them.

One night, as Ianto was lying awake in bed, he heard the fair folk downstairs, and one of them said to the others "I wish we had some bread and cheese on this cold and frosty night, but the poor man has only a morsel left; and though it's true that would be a good meal for us, it is but a mouthful to him, and he might starve if we took it." At this Ianto, feeling generous, yelled at the top of his voice "Take anything I've got in the cupboard, and you're welcome to it!" Then he turned over and went to sleep.

When he went down to the kitchen next morning, he looked into the cupboard to see if there might be a bit of a crust left, but no sooner had he opened the door than he cried out in amazement, for there stood the finest cheese he had ever seen in his life, with two loaves of freshly-baked crusty bread. Ianto knew that this was the doing of the fairies, so he waved his hand towards the wood where they lived and exclaimed "Good luck to you, my friends!" And no sooner had he finished speaking than he saw a silver shilling on the hob.

After that, every morning when Ianto got up there would be a new silver shilling on the hob, and new bread and cheese in the cupboard. So Ianto was able to afford good beer and good tobacco when he went out of an evening, and all the neighbours were amazed how well fed and well off he was, although they never saw him do a stroke of work. He had enough to keep his wife in ease and comfort too, and he was given the nickname of Lucky Ianto.

And so his good fortune might have continued if it had not been for the nagging of his wife Betsi. She would give him no peace until she could find out where the bread and cheese and silver shillings came from. In reply to her questions, Ianto said one day "Now then, dear wife, you know that if I tell you I will never get any more money or food." Then Betsi knew that the fair folk were responsible. "Aha" she said, "then it's the fairies!" And Ianto replied, without thinking, "Dammo! Yes the fairies it is," and he thrust his hands in his trouser pockets and went out of the house in a sulk.

As he went out of the door he had seven silver shillings in his pocket, but he felt for the coins he realised that they had disappeared. And from that day on, having given away his secret, Ianto received no more silver shillings from the *Tylwyth Teg*.

Date : c 1820   Source : Sikes p.123

4.9 The Great Black Snake of Presely

Once upon a time a great black snake inhabited a certain part of the Presely Hills. Sometimes it would be seen coiled in the sunshine, fast asleep. When it lay thus its head and tail did not quite meet, and in the middle of the coil there was a pile of treasure - gold and silver goblets, jewellery and copper coins. Many people saw this treasure and its fearsome guardian, but nobody dared to take it.

One day a working man came upon the black snake and its treasure while walking in the hills. He resolved to take just a little of the treasure without waking the serpent, so he walked through the gap between its head and its tail and then stopped, fearsome lest it should wake. But the snake slumbered on, and the man became more confident. He began to fill his pockets with gold, silver and copper coins. When the pockets were full he decided to take just a little more, so he took off his jacket, laid it on the grass, and began to pile more treasures on top of it.

But in his eagerness the man forgot all about the snake, and suddenly he was frightened out of his wits by a fearsome roar. He fled through the gap between head and tale, leaving his coat and the treasure behind him. He was unharmed, but when he dared to stop and look back he caught a last glimpse of the snake and its treasure sinking into the mountainside, accompanied by a mighty roaring sound. At last the snake disappeared, and it was never seen again.

Date : c 1825   *Source : Trevelyan p.176*

4.10 The Mermaid at Porth-y-Rhaw

The wild north coast of the St David's Peninsula (Dewisland) is, it seems, especially suitable for mermaids, and there are a number of stories of encounters with these fair creatures. The sea captain Daniel Huws was certain that he saw a whole mermaid town beneath the waves off Trefin when he was becalmed there during a voyage in 1858. And there is another story of an encounter in June 1780 between some quarry-men from Penbiri and a mermaid at the nearby creek of Porth-y-Rhaw.

It so happened that the "rockmen" made a habit of going down to the seaside for their lunch on fine summer days. On this particular day the light was bright and clear, and the sea surface was as placid as a lake. Suddenly the rockmen noticed a figure sitting on a rock close to the base of the cliffs, and they realised that she was a *gwenhudwy* or mermaid. She was quite preoccupied with combing her long golden hair, and the men noticed that above the waist she was "like the lasses of Wales", while below she had the body of a fish. They managed to get close enough to talk to her, and discovered that she understood Welsh. They attempted to open a conversation with her, but all she would say to them was this: "Reaping in Pembrokeshire and weeding in Carmarthenshire." Then she slipped off the rock and disappeared down into the azure depths, leaving the rockmen to puzzle over the meaning of what she had said.

Date : 1780   *Source : Rhys, p.165*

4.11 A Water Horse at Nolton

The *ceffyl dwr* was a small, beautiful horse which tempted unwary travellers to ride but which had a nasty habit of suddenly galloping off towards the water, either throwing off its riders in the process or taking them down into the shadowy depths. It had a healthy respect only for ministers of religion, who were generally allowed to ride in peace and safety.

Once upon a time a water horse was seen by a local farmer upon the beach at Nolton Haven after a mighty storm. It was a beautiful creature, dappled like the lights and shades of a summer woodland, and it stood quite still while the farmer caught it. It was a fine sturdy animal and the farmer harnessed it to his plough and used it for his ploughing for several weeks. One day, however, while ploughing in a field adjacent to the coast, the horse suddenly smelt the salt tang of the sea and rushed off towards the water, dragging both plough and ploughman with it across the field and over the cliff. Neither the horse, nor the plough, nor the ploughman, were ever seen again.

Date : c 1750 ?   *Source : Roberts p.25*

4.12 The Mermaid of Carregwastad

There is an interesting story of a mermaid who was caught in the early 1700s by a group of men on the cliffs at Carregwastad, quite close to the site where the French invasion force landed some decades later.

The men all came from one farm not far from Llanwnda. We do not know how they captured the mermaid, but she was carried, protesting bitterly from the cliffs to the farm, where she was locked up in one of the rooms. There she stayed for some time, but at last she became greatly distressed, and begged to be allowed to return to "the Brine Land". The men were reluctant to let her go, for she was very beautiful, and was quite a novelty to show to their friends. But at last she promised to give the householders three bits of advice if they would release her. At last, overwhelmed by her tearful entreaties, the family agreed to the bargain and agreed to take her back to the sea. True to her word, before she slipped into the water the mermaid passed on her three advices. The first one was as follows: "Skim the surface of the potage before adding sweet milk to it; it will be whiter and sweeter, and less of it will do."

The other two advices have never been revealed, but it is said that the family, after releasing the mermaid back to the sea, have followed them to this day, and have profited greatly from them. We still do not know the name of the farmer, nor the name of the farm, but if you look for the wealthiest farm in the Llanwnda district, you may be sure that this is the farm which is still benefiting from the encounter with the mermaid.

Date : c 1730   *Source : Rhys p.165*

4.13 The Old Man in the Cradle

It was the month of June, and the sun was high in the afternoon sky as the good people of Cenarth pressed on with their hay-making. It was almost too hot to work, but the hay harvest had to be finished before the weather broke, and every able-bodied person was out on the hay-meadows.

Elen wanted to help too, so she left her one-year-old baby son in his wicker-work cradle in the coolness of the kitchen and set off for the meadow, content in the knowledge that the child was watched over her ancient and kindly neighbour Sarah. The old lady was well over eighty years old, and did not see too well, but after a little while she heard the baby crying. So she shouted down to the hay-field for Elen to return, and within a couple of minutes the mother was back to console her child. She picked the baby up out of the cradle and nursed him to her breast, saying "Don't cry, cariad, your mam is here!"

But then she noticed, to her great consternation, that the baby looked different. In fact, he had the face of an old man. Elen was first of all confused and then panic-stricken, so as calmly as she could she replaced the child in the cradle and ran out to call her neighbours from the hay meadow.

After much discussion the old lady from next door, and the other neighbours, all agreed that it was a child of *Rhys Ddwfn* (in other words, a fairy) who was in the cradle, and not her own dearly beloved child. It was decided that the only person who could retreive the child was the *hudol* or sorcerer from Newcastle Emlyn, and one of the men volunteered to saddle up his pony and gallop off the fetch him. At last the sorcerer arrived, and looked at the child. "Aha!" he said. "I have seen his like before. He is indeed one of the little people, and he is exactly the same age as the baby's grandfather. It will be a hard job to get rid of him, but I have dealt with more difficult matters. So let us see what we can do."

With that, he instructed one of the Cenarth lads to fetch a shovel. Then it was placed in the kitchen fire (which was never allowed to go out, no matter how warm the weather) until it was red hot. Then the sorcerer took the shovel by the handle and held it in front of the baby's face. In an instant, a short, hairy old man leapt out of the cot and took to his heels, and all eyes followed him as he rushed off down the road to Abercuch. He was never seen in the district again; but miraculously, as soon as Elen looked back at her baby's cradle she saw that the child was there, fast asleep, and none the worse for his experience.

Date : c 1830?   Source : Rhys, p 162

4.14 The Little People near Puncheston

Some years ago a freelance radio reporter was travelling around north Pembrokeshire with his tape recorder, making a programme for the BBC about the supernatural. He interviewed many people in and around Cwm Gwaun, and found that the area abounded with strange tales.

He was advised to go and visit an old bachelor farmer who lived in the remote hills near Puncheston, and turned up at the farm in order to record an interview. The farmer told the reporter that his farm was populated with "The Little People". He said that they were rather mischievous, but that he had learned to live with them and that they did not cause him any great trouble. The reporter asked if he could have a tour of the farm, so the two of them set off to walk around the buildings and fields, recording their conversation on the tape recorder. Soon they came to a rough field in the valley below the farm, and as the farmer opened the gate he said "Watch out for the little buggers in here. They are always up to mischief, and there's no knowing what they will get up to next."

They closed the gate behind them, walked around the field for a while, and eventually left again by the same gate. All the while the reporter and the farmer were chatting into the microphone, and all the while the tape recorder was running. At last the reporter completed his interview, and set off for home. After supper he decided to check over his tapes, and on listening to the recording of his conversation with the old bachelor farmer he found that the sound quality was excellent. However, he was amazed to discover that the tape was blank from the moment that the two of them had entered the bottom field until the moment that they left. After that, the sound quality of the recording was once again perfect. He rang up the old farmer to report the inexplicable loss of part of the interview, but the old man roared with laughter. "Dammo," he said. "I knew we'd have trouble in the bottom field. Those little buggers have been at it again....."

Date: 1979   Source: word of mouth

4.15 The Water Boy at Penyholt Bay

Around the middle of the eighteenth century Mr Henry Reynolds farmed the land around Penyholt Bay and Linney Head, on the limestone coast of the Castlemartin peninsula. One calm morning he went down to the cliffs and he was surprised to see a figure on the surface of the water. He knew the water to be very deep at that point, and so he crept closer to investigate. From a distance of about ten yards, he had an excellent view of a youth aged about 16, with very pale skin. The boy was moving about in the water, and Mr Reynolds saw that he had a long brown tail which moved from side to side as he swam. Above the waist his body was quite normal, but he had rather short and thick arms and hands. He had coarse ribbon-like hair which fell down his back. He made no sounds, and his facial expression was "wild and fierce". Mr Reynolds sat looking at the water boy for about an hour, and then decided to run home to the farm and fetch his wife. When they returned to Penyholt Bay the boy had gone.

Date: c 1750   Source: Roberts p 51

PEMBROKESHIRE FOLK TALES

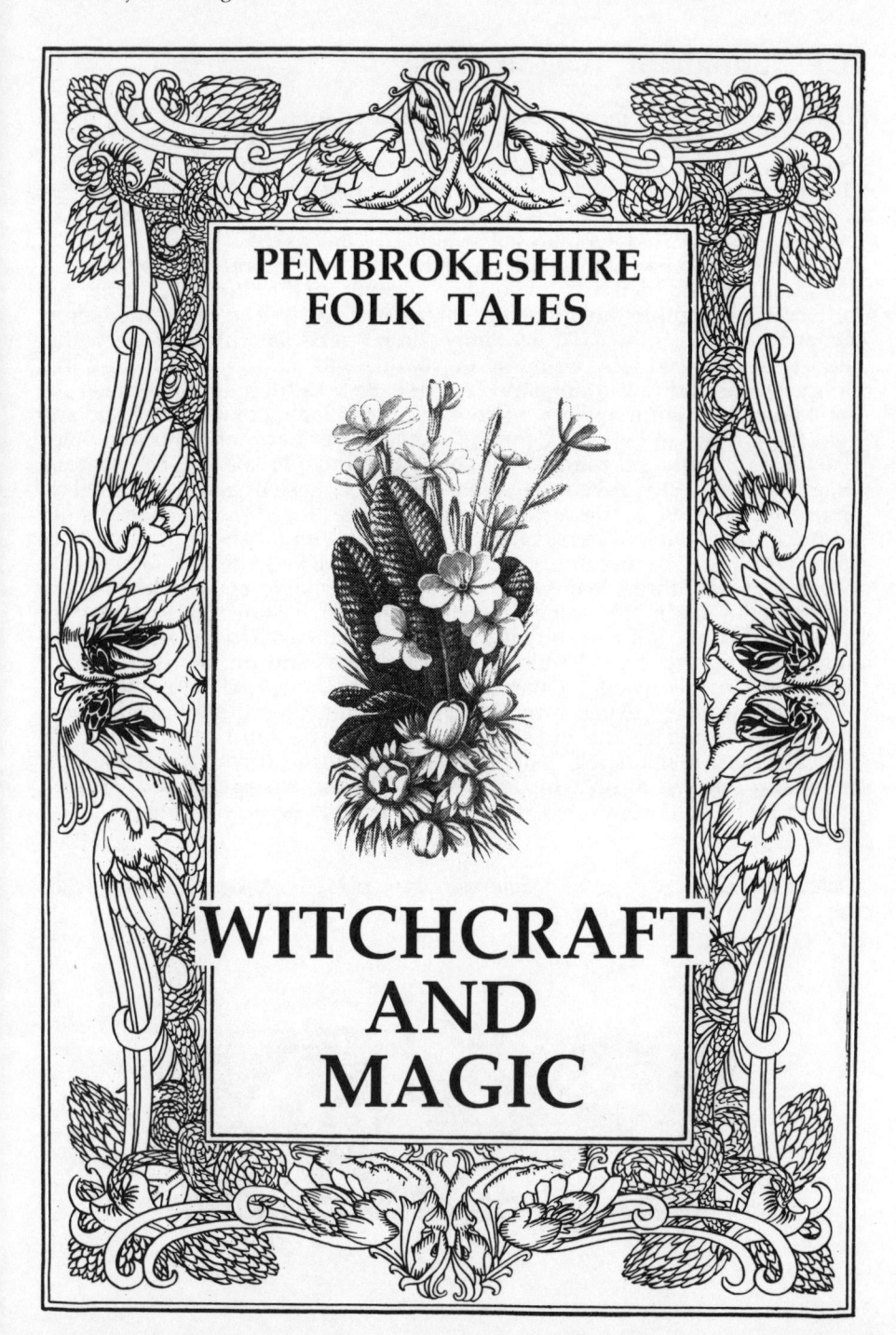

WITCHCRAFT AND MAGIC

5.1 Hannah of Walton West

Once upon a time a farmer and his young daughter were travelling home by horse and cart towards Little Haven, having been to the fair at Haverfordwest. The little girl was fast asleep in the cart as it rattled along the rough road towards the setting sun. As they approached Walton West a gnarled old woman in a long black shawl appeared by the roadside. "Can you give a tired old woman a lift home?" she asked.

The farmer knew her as old Hannah, who was reported to be a witch (*gwyddon*). He nodded and invited her to climb up into the cart, for there is no point in tempting fate by being unkind to a witch. The cart rattled along for another mile or so, and suddenly the farmer's daughter awoke with a start to see the old lady wringing her hands and muttering to herself in a language she did not understand. At first she was frightened, because she too knew that Hannah was a witch; but the old lady looked quite kind and told the girl not to be afraid, for she would never harm an innocent child.

At last the little girl plucked up enough courage to speak. "Do you cast magic spells?" she asked. Hannah merely chuckled and continued to mumble to herself as the cart lurched along the rutted track. Then the girl spotted three teams of horses harrowing a field, under the control of three farm workers. She became mischievous, and asked the old lady if she could stop the three teams of horses with a magic spell. Old Hannah whispered some more strange words, and in an instant the first team of horses shied up as if confronted by a wall of flame. Then the second team shied up, causing the farm-boy to drop the reins and flee across the field. The third team carried on harrowing as if nothing had happened.

The girl watched expectantly, but Hannah appeared quite unconcerned. Then she turned to the girl and explained. "The third team cannot be affected by a magic spell," she said, "because the driver has a piece of mountain ash tied to his whip, and mountain ash has special properties."

And so the cart continued to rattle and rumble its way towards Walton West.

Date : c 1800 ?   *Sources : Davies p.241, Roberts p.23, Radford p.81*

5.2 Sally-Anne of Trefelyn

Sally-Anne was a shy, dark-haired girl who lived with her grandmother not far from Mathry. She was a lonely child, for the cottage where she lived was isolated in a deep valley, and there were few visitors because her grandmother was thought by the locals to be a witch or *gwyddon*.

Sally-Anne worked on a farm called Trefelyn, just outside the village, and she walked there every morning at dawn. She had many farm duties, but she loved the animals so much that she quite neglected her work in the farmhouse on washing, cleaning, cooking and mending. The farmer's wife frequently had to hunt for her all over the farm, where she would invariably be found in the company of the sheep or cattle. She was reproached time and again, but when she did not mend her ways she was finally summoned to the farmer, who dismissed her and sent her on her way back to her grandmother. "And don't ever come back again!" he shouted angrily as tears welled up in her eyes.

"But the animals will fret terribly without me," she pleaded. "They need me to be with them." But the farmer remained unmoved, and the dejected child walked back across the fields to her cottage.

When she arrived and tearfully told her grandmother that she had lost her job the old woman was furious, for the small wages and rations of milk, butter and eggs were all they had to live on. For the rest of the day grandmother sat in her rocking-chair, stroking her black cat and muttering quietly to herself; and there she remained until far into the night.

Next morning, back on the farm, the farmer found the bull in a furious temper and the cows lowing and tugging at their chains and refusing to cooperate during milking. The cocks were fighting and the hens stopped laying. Many of the sheep and lambs broke out through the hedges and wandered off across fields belong to neighbouring farms. No matter what the farmer did, he could not control the animals, and by the evening he was getting seriously worried. "I have never seen anything like it," he said. "It is as if a strange spell has come over them."

That evening, at the little cottage, Sally-Anne and her grandmother sat quietly in the candle-light. The girl was still very upset at the loss of her job but the old woman placed a hand on her shoulder. "Don't fret, child," she said. "As likely as not, you'll soon hear a knock on the door, and before the week is out you'll be back with your animals at Trefelyn."

And so it was that next day the farmer arrived and begged Sally-Anne to come and work on the farm again.....

Date : c 1850 ?   *Source : Radford p.103*

5.3 The Old Black Witch of Cwmslade

Not waiting to see what had happened to the phantom dog, they both fled.

Cwmslade was a small and very ancient cottage not far from Tufton, located on land which is now devoted to forestry. At the time of this story, during the Second World War, there was an American garrison at Puncheston, and over the mountain of Mynydd Castlebythe it was possible to see and hear the American army tanks firing at their targets.

Around 1943 an Englishman named Ron Stevens lived in the cottage and used it for training hawks; and in the holidays he was helped by John, a twelve-year-old Welsh lad.

One day the pair were feeding the hawks on raw rabbit meat in the little garden at the back of the cottage. Suddenly the lad noticed that the thick thorn hedge around the garden was moving. The hawks became alarmed, and as Ron Stevens and the boy tried to calm them down a huge black dog, standing about four feet high at the shoulder, appeared to walk straight through the hedge, which was normally quite impenetrable. Ron told the boy to chase the dog away, and as he rose a strange old woman appeared straight in front of him.

The witch (*gwyddon*) had a black hat on her head, and her white teeth curled right out over her bottom lip. She was about the same height as Dick. Her clothes were all black, and her hands were encased as though in gloves and folded across her chest. She wore battered black boots, with the toes curled up. There was an ancient enigmatic smile on her face, and she walked slowly out of the garden, beckoning for Ron and the lad to follow. This they did, walking as if in a trance. Afterwards they noticed that they had been unable to talk at this time. The old woman led them through a gap in the thorn hedge towards a well, and there she disappeared.

Ron and the boy, still mesmerised, looked into the well, but the water was perfectly still. Nothing stirred. Then they were released from the spell. Not waiting to see what had happened to the phantom dog, they both fled. John ran home, straight across the bog whereas normally he skirted round it. When he arrived home he was totally exhausted, covered in mud, and still in a state of shock. He collapsed on the passage floor in front of his mother, and for a fortnight afterwards he was too ill to get out of bed. Ron Stevens was so frightened by the episode that he moved out of the cottage the same evening, never to return. Not long afterwards the cottage was demolished to make way for forestry work, and the site is now lost in the dark shadows of the coniferous woodland.

Date : 1943 *Source : Gwyndaf 1977, Brooks p.82-3*

5.4 The Servant Girl of Gelli-fawr

The members of a well-known Gwaun Valley family were noted for their knowledge of witchcraft. It so happened that they applied to become members of Caersalem Chapel in Cilgwyn. However, one of their number could not resist casting a spell or *cyfaredd* on the very day that she was baptised. She bewitched a young servant girl of Gelli-fawr farm while sitting behind her in the chapel. In the middle of the service, the poor girl rushed out of her pew, and out of the chapel, and ran wildly about the roads of Cilgwyn. This continued for several days. Her father, having tried every means of pacifying her, went at last to Cwrt-y-Cadno in Carmarthenshire to consult Dr Harries, the well-known *dyn hysbys* or wise man. Dr Harries asked no questions, but accurately told her father what had happened and even showed him the scene all over again in a mirror. He then gave him a piece of paper with some mysterious words written on it, which the girl had to wear on her breast. And this was quite sufficient to break the spell and to bring the poor girl back to normal again. Afterwards she had no recollection of what had happened, but continued with her duties on the farm.

Date : c 1810 *Sources : Davies p.231, Roberts p.15*

Afterwards she had no recollection of what had happened, but continued with her duties on the farm.

5.5 Abe Biddle and the Hornets

At the beginning of the last century there was a soothsayer or *dyn hysbys* called Dr Joseph Harries, otherwise known as Abe Biddle of Werndew, near Dinas. (Sometimes in old books he is confused with Billy Biddle, a famous fiddler, who came from Jeffreyston near Tenby; but so far as we know he was no relation.) Abe was well known for his remarkable powers and for his ability as a healer. He could foretell the future, but he also had a mastery of the occult. Although he was best known in the Fishguard-Newport area his fame spread all over Pembrokeshire and even further afield.

During the winter of 1803 there was an evening party for gentlemen in a north Pembrokeshire vicarage. There were many clergymen and their guests present, and a good time was had by all, with fine food, singing, telling of tales and much laughter. At last, in the early hours, the conversation drifted round to the occult. Abe Biddle said nothing, for his strange powers were well known, but one elderly cleric denounced all sorcery and witchcraft (*rheibio*), and of course it was incumbent upon all the other clerics present to nod gravely in agreement.

At last Abe Biddle got up, disappeared through the French doors onto the lawn, and returned holding three small rings. He held them up, saying quietly to the assembled company "Now, gentlemen, we'll see what is possible." He placed the three rings on the floor, left the room and locked the door on the outside, leaving the trapped clerics and their guests to stare intently at the rings. Suddenly, in one of the rings, a small buzzing insect appeared. As the men watched it grew and grew into a large angry hornet. It flew into another ring and was replaced by a second fly in the first ring. This also turned into a huge hornet. As they watched with mounting alarm the process speeded up until the room was filled with droning hornets. Eventually the ceiling was darkened with the creatures and panic set in as they flew into men's hair and clothes, into the curtains and furniture. As the men shouted and fought to escape from the room Abe Biddle suddenly opened the door. In an instant the hornets swarmed out towards the darkness and droned away into the distance. Abe Biddle said nothing, but picked the rings up off the floor. He knew that he had spoiled the party, but thereafter all the clerics present became somewhat more cautious in their pronouncements concerning matters beyond their understanding.

Date : 1803   *Sources : Roberts p.20, Trevelyan p.218*

5.6 Unpleasantness at Orielton

Some of the earliest folk tales of Pembrokeshire are to be found in the writings of Giraldus Cambrensis, an inveterate twelfth-century recorder of tit-bits of information. This tale is about the grand house of Orielton, now a Field Studies Centre but then much smaller and simpler in appearance. In 1190 the house belonged to one Stephen Wiriet. It appears that a curse had been placed upon the house, for the poor man and his family and friends were greatly troubled by an "unclean spirit". In Welsh, such a spirit would have been called a *bwgan*.

The spirit threw dirt at people, "more with a view of mockery than of injury", but also conversed quite freely with visitors. Apparently it also had strange powers, for it could look into past history in a way that was somewhat embarrassing. According to Giraldus, in reply to the taunts and curses of visitors, the spirit "upraided them openly with everything that they had done from their birth, and which they were not willing should be heard or known by others". Stephen Wiriet sought to exorcise the spirit from the house by invoking the help of various clerics, but the place could not be purified that easily, for the spirit appeared unaffected by the sprinkling of holy water or by religious ceremony. Even worse, the priests themselves, although supposedly protected by the crucifix and by holy water and although greatly respected as devout men of God, were "equally subject to the same insults".

Giraldus related that the bewitching of the house was so severe that poor Stephen Wiriet was eventually reduced from affluence "to poverty and distress" as the Orielton estate fell upon hard times.

Date : c 1190   Sources : Giraldus p.151, Roberts p.28

5.7 The Bewitched Cottage

For as long as she could remember, the old lady had lived in a tiny cottage near the Pembrokeshire border. She probably thought it was her own, but in fact it was part of an estate belonging to Whitland Abbey. But she was happy there. She kept herself very much to herself, and she was renowned for her ability to foretell the future and for her vast knowledge of medicinal herbs.

In the year 1879 she received a very nasty shock, when a young man knocked on her door with a message from the landlord of the estate. He was just an estate worker, he explained, but he had been told to call on her and inform her that the estate had been sold. The new owner was intent upon selling all the estate cottages. This meant that she would have to move out and find somewhere else to live. Naturally enough, the old lady became furious at this; she stamped her foot and ranted and raved and then screamed at the young man "Just you wait! When I leave my cottage some very unpleasant things will happen to everybody who has a hand in this, and that means you too!"

The poor young man felt very uncomfortable at this, since he was simply doing as his master had told him. But he went off home and forgot all about it. Before long the old woman managed to find another cottage and moved away from the Whitland Abbey estate with her meagre possessions.

Shortly after the cottage became empty, the unpleasant things which she had predicted began to happen. The innocent young messenger was the first to suffer, for his wife gave birth to a terribly deformed baby which died when it was only one day old. Then the man who bought the cottage was taken ill as soon as he moved in, and his ailment mystified all the doctors who were consulted. He never recovered, and was unable to walk for the rest of his life. Soon the locals were all convinced that there was a curse upon the cottage.

Finally the old woman's curse began to affect the local doctor, who was the brother of the man who brought her old home. His cows, pigs and horses all seemed to be bewitched, for they all suffered from fits and failed to respond to treatment. One by one, the animals all died. Strangely enough, the new owner of Whitland Abbey, who had been responsible for selling the cottage in the first place, was never affected by the curse, and nor did his animals suffer any ill-effects.

Date : 1879   *Source : Pugh p.86*

5.8 The Launch of HMS "Lion"

...she returned to her cottage and settled down to a nice cup of tea.

In the heyday of the Royal Naval Dockyard at Pembroke Dock the launch of each new ship was accompanied by celebration on a grand scale. Normally the reserved seats were in great demand, kept for local dignitaries, officers and their families.

In the year 1847 the time came to launch HMS **Lion,** the largest warship in the Royal Navy. This was a highly prestigious event, and competition for reserved seating was intense. When the great day arrived a strange old woman known as Betty Foggy came up to the Dockyard gate and asked to be given one of the reserved seats where she could listen to the speeches and see the breaking of the bottle on the ship's bows. But she was greeted with derision and told to go away. "In that case", she said, "there will be no launch today. You may all go home, good people." And off she went into the town, where she returned to her cottage and settled down to a nice cup of tea.

The **Lion** was duly named, and the champagne broken on her bows. The dogshores were knocked away, but the vessel refused to budge. No matter what the Dockyard workers did to induce the vessel to move down the slipway, she remained firmly stuck. Eventually, to the embarrassment of the Dockyard officials, all the guests had to go off home. And the **Lion** remained immovable on the slipway until the next high tide came round, when she slid into the water without the slightest trouble.

Date : 1847   Sources : Davies p.237, Bielski p.44

5.9 Adam of Roch Castle

The tall tower of Roch Castle, perched on its volcanic crag, dominates the landscape around the north-eastern corner of St Bride's Bay. It marks the northernmost extent of Norman influence in this part of Pembrokeshire, and stands at the western end of the Landsker. The lordship which it controlled was remote and vulnerable to attack by the Welsh princes, and the castle was never built to its original design. Only the stone keep was completed and the lack of further progress on the building work may have been due to the sad and premature demise of the builder, Adam de la Roche.

. . . only the stone keep was completed.

Adam was the first feudal Norman lord of Roch in the twelfth century. One winters day he was cursed by a *gwyddon* or witch, who said that before a year would pass, he would die from the bite of an adder. Now adders were quite common in the dry places around the castle keep, and Adam became very fearful for his life. Soon he was so affected by the witch's curse that he shut himself away in the topmost room of the tower, refusing to come down even in bad weather when it was most unlikely that he would encounter an adder. All his food and clothing and firewood had to be brought up to him as he lived the life of a recluse. As the seasons passed he began to relax a little, and after Christmas the tower was buffeted again by the storms of a typical Pembrokeshire winter.

With only one day to go until the end of the curse, Adam began to feel that he would survive. It was a bitterly cold evening, and as the light faded he ordered his old servant woman to bring up a new bundle of firewood from the store so that he could keep a good blaze going in his hearth overnight. This she did, and after stoking up the fire Adam settled down before its warmth and fell asleep. But unknown to both the old woman and her master, an adder had chosen to hibernate in the bundles of firewood stowed outside, and had been carried up with the sticks into Adam's room. As the warmth spread around the room the adder woke from its hibernation.

And so it was that when the servants came up to Adam's room next morning they found their master dead, poisoned by the bite of an adder as the old witch had foretold.

Date : c 1130 ? *Sources : Roberts p.21, Fenton p.82*

5.10 Wil Tiriet and the College Principal

Around 1830-1850 there was in the hamlet of Caerfarchell, near Middle Mill, a tailor called William Howells. He was widely known as Wil Tiriet or Wiliet, and he had special powers. In Welsh he was known as a *dyn hysbys* or soothsayer, and two stories survive which reveal how he could look into the future. This is the first story.

The old Baptist chapel at Middle Mill had a large congregation at that time - large enough to demand the pastoral care of two ministers. The older of the two, John Reynolds, was well known in Baptist circles throughout West Wales; his young assistant was called William Jones. One day Wil Tiriet prophesied that the younger man would soon die, and the prophecy soon became public knowledge. The whole community was thrown into confusion by this prediction - some people were outraged, some were terrified, some were angry, and others were sceptical. As if in answer to those who professed not to believe him, Wil Tiriet further prophesied that at the funeral of William Jones there would be a minister with a very long white beard. Since nobody knew of a white-bearded minister in the district everybody assumed that Wil's eerie predictions could not possibly come true.

In a few weeks William Jones was dead. On the day of the funeral the cortege started from the young minister's house and made its slow way to the chapel. They arrived and entered, and there, sitting in the big pew, was a reverend gentleman with a long white beard. It transpired that he was Dr Thomas Davies, the principal of the Haverfordwest Baptist College, who had rushed on horseback to the funeral. He had lost much time because his horse had cast a shoe; and so, being too late to attend the gathering at the house of the deceased, he had gone straight to the chapel ahead of the rest of the mourners.

Date : c 1840   *Sources : Pembs Mag 53, T.G. Jones, p.28*

5.11 Wil Tiriet and the Nolton Coffin

Once upon a time, about 1830, Wil Tiriet of Caerfarchell was chatting to one of his neighbours, a carpenter named Francis John. He told him that there would soon be a funeral of a young man at Fachelich, a hamlet about two miles away. The carpenter laughed at him, for none of the young men of Fachelich was known to be ill, but the soothsayer insisted "Thou'llt believe it when thy brother and thou carry his coffin past the doctor's house on the road to Fachelich." The matter was quickly forgotten.

Then there came a report of a sailor being drowned near Nolton Haven, whose body had been washed ashore. The dead man proved to be from Fachelich, and Francis John and his brother Bill were asked to make the coffin. They had to carry the coffin to Nolton, and then back to Fachelich with the body inside. It was a long walk, and the coffin was heavy, and having remembered Wil Tiriet's prophecy Francis determined to prove him wrong by getting two other neighbours to give a hand. The men were to take it turn and turn about, but there was some confusion and in the argument about whose turn was next Wil's prophecy was forgotten about. Sure enough, when the coffin was carried past the doctor's door it was carried by Francis and Bill, with the other two men walking behind.

Date : 1830   Source : T.G. Jones p.28

Then there came a report of a sailor being drowned near Nolton Haven, whose body had been washed ashore.

5.12 The Bewitching at Walton East

Around 1850 there was an old woman in Walton East who was supposed to be a witch (*gwyddon*). One day two young women, daughters of a local farmer and his wife, were suddenly taken ill. It was widely assumed that the old woman had bewitched them, so the girls' mother went to her cottage and rebuked her with the words "Old woman! Why did you bewitch my daughters? Come and undo thy wickedness!"

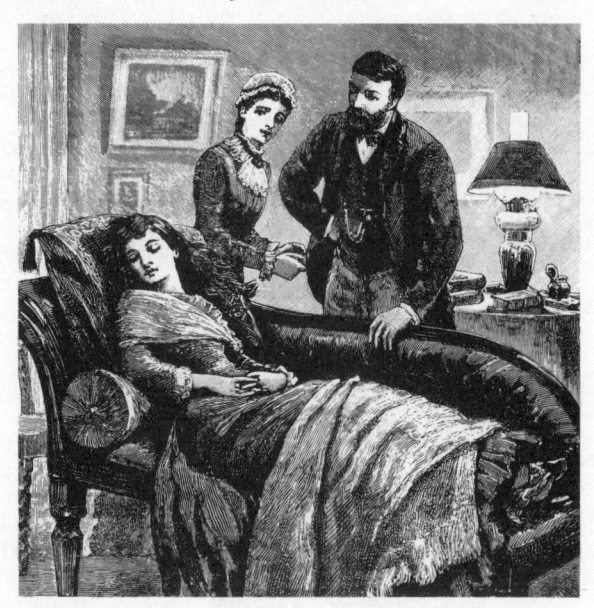

......*the daughter who had not heard the release from the spell continued to be ill, and her condition even deteriorated.*

The old woman denied that she had anything to do with the illness, but the mother would not believe her protestations and compelled her to come to the farmhouse. When they reached the front door of the house the mother forced the old witch to say "God bless thee." The girls were in bed in an upstairs room at the time, but only one of them heard the old women's words. She immediately recovered from her illness. However, the daughter who had not heard the release from the spell continued to be ill, and her condition even deteriorated. For fifteen years she refused to leave her bedroom and behaved very strangely. When anybody entered the room she hid under the bed-clothes like a rat, and she refused to eat her meals in the presence of anybody else.

At last the old woman died, and immediately the sick daughter started to recover. As the mortal remains of the witch decayed in the grave she became better and better, until she was completely well again.

Later, the young woman married a wealthy local farmer. She lived a perfectly normal and fulfilling life in the Walton East area, and enjoyed the very best of health.

Date : c 1850   *Source : Davies p.234*

5.13 John Jenkin and the Evil Spirits

John Jenkin was a schoolmaster in Pembrokeshire in the early years of the nineteenth century, but he was best known in his local community as a conjuror or *consuriwr* who was able to make contact with the Devil and his evil spirits.

One day one of Mr Jenkin's pupils asked him whether it would be possible for him to see the Devil. "You may see him", said the master, "if you have the courage for it. But I do not choose to call him until I have work for him to do." So the boy waited. Not long afterwards, a man came to the master; he reported the theft of some money, and asked if he could help him to identify the culprit. "Now," said the master to the pupil, "I have some work for him."

Next night, John Jenkin led the boy out into the wood and drew a circle on the ground, so that they both stood inside the circle. Then the master called an evil spirit by its name. A light appeared in the sky, and it shot like a bolt of lightning down to the circle. Then, as it moved around the outside of the circle, the conjuror asked it who had stolen the man's money; the evil spirit replied that it did not know, and disappeared. Then the schoolmaster called another evil spirit by name; and presently they saw the resemblance of a bull flying through the air, as fierce and ferocious as could be imagined, and it too landed outside the circle. The mighty beast was asked who had stolen the money, but it did not know; and so it too disappeared.

By now the boy was almost fainting with fright, and the schoolmaster waited considerately for a while for him to recover his wits. Then he called for a third spirit. This time a spirit dressed in white came out of the shadows of the wood, and moved quietly around the circle. "Ah," said the conjuror, "this is better! Now we shall get to the bottom of this." And sure enough, the spirit spoke to the master in a language the boy did not understand. Then it disappeared in a ball of red fire.

After this, John Jenkin correctly told the man who had stolen his money, and it was recovered. But apparently the boy was so frightened by the encounter with the evil spirits that he was in poor health for many years afterwards.

The mighty beast was asked who had stolen the money, but it did not know....

Date : c 1820 ?
Source : Sikes p.199

5.14 Abe Biddle and the Missing Jewels

Abe Biddle (otherwise known as Dr Harries) was once called in by a lady of some social standing who was staying at the mansion of a wealthy Pembrokeshire family. The doctor duly arrived, and impressed the lady with his appearance. He was a tall, slender man with long shaggy hair and large, deep-set eyes, and a somewhat dreamy expression on his face. But his voice was well modulated and his manner courteous, and this gave the lady some confidence that he might be able to help her with a matter that required some discretion.

The countess described to Abe Biddle how she had lost some of her jewels, and she declared that they had been safely in her travelling bag when she had left another Pembrokeshire mansion at dawn the previous day. On hearing the story Abe Biddle opened his battered old bag and took out a mirror, which he placed on the table in front of the countess. Then he asked her to look into it and to tell him what she saw. She sat down and looked into the mirror while Abe Biddle asked her to "compose herself". At last she said that she could see nothing but a mist, which she described as like the steam from a boiler. "Look again", said the good doctor. And as she looked quietly into the mirror the mist rolled away and she saw a woman in a dress of white brocade, with her back turned towards her. "Do you know her?" asked Abe. "I don't think so," replied the Countess, "but I cannot see her face, for her back is turned." The doctor then told her to pause for a while, and to close her eyes. This she did. After a few minutes she was asked to open her eyes again and to look once more into the mirror.

And now, as the countess looked, the woman in the mirror turned to face her, and she was amazed to see some of her jewels in her hands, and others upon her neck and in her hair. Again Abe Biddle asked "Do you know her?" And the countess instantly recognized her as a personal friend of her hostess, from whom she had recently taken her leave.

Abe Biddle was asked to undertake discreet investigations, which he did with considerable tact. The result was the restoration of the jewels to their rightful owner. The thief was never prosecuted, but the solving of the mystery made a profound impression upon a small circle of the Pembrokeshire gentry.

Date : 1810   Source : Trevelyan p.219

5.15 The Troublesome Hare of Pontfaen

Mr Griffiths of Maenclochog once related how his mother encountered a troublesome witch when she was young. At the time (around 1820) she worked at the squire's house at Pontfaen, and whenever she went out in the morning to milk the cows she was greatly bothered by a hare. The animal pranced about and disturbed the cows, so that they became difficult to milk. She knew that the hare was really an old witch called Maggie who lived in the neighbourhood, and at last she complained to her master.

Next morning when she went out to milk the cows the squire came with her, and shot at the hare. Somehow the animal escaped, but the shot had wounded it and drawn blood. They watched it limping away into the undergrowth, leaving a trail of blood on the grass. Now the servant girl was happy, since a witch loses her power immediately on the drawing of blood. Sure enough, the girl was not bothered by the hare any more. Soon afterwards she decided to call on old Maggie to see how she was, and she found her in bed, feeling not at all well, with her leg all bandaged up.

Date : c 1820   *Source : Davies p.242*

5.16 The Black Calf of Narberth

In the last century a black calf was often seen by old people in the vicinity of Narberth, and it was reputed to be the devil in disguise. Somewhat enigmatically, the devil would always be referred to as "The Old Gentleman". Often the calf would be seen near a certain brook on the road to Cold Blow, but as the seasons and years passed it never changed in appearance or grew any larger. Some local people decided to investigate the phenomenon, refusing to believe that all of the reports of the black calf could refer to the same animal; but when they enquired of all the farmers in the neighbourhood whether there were any calves missing, they all replied that their calves were safely shut in with their other animals.

The black calf continued to appear near the brook, but at last one smart farmer managed to catch it. He took it home and shut it in the cowshed with his other cattle; but when he came to let the animals out the next morning the calf had gone. After this the calf continued to be seen at intervals by many people, old and young, in the Narberth area.

Date : c 1850 ?   *Sources : Trevelyan p.152, Davies p.181*

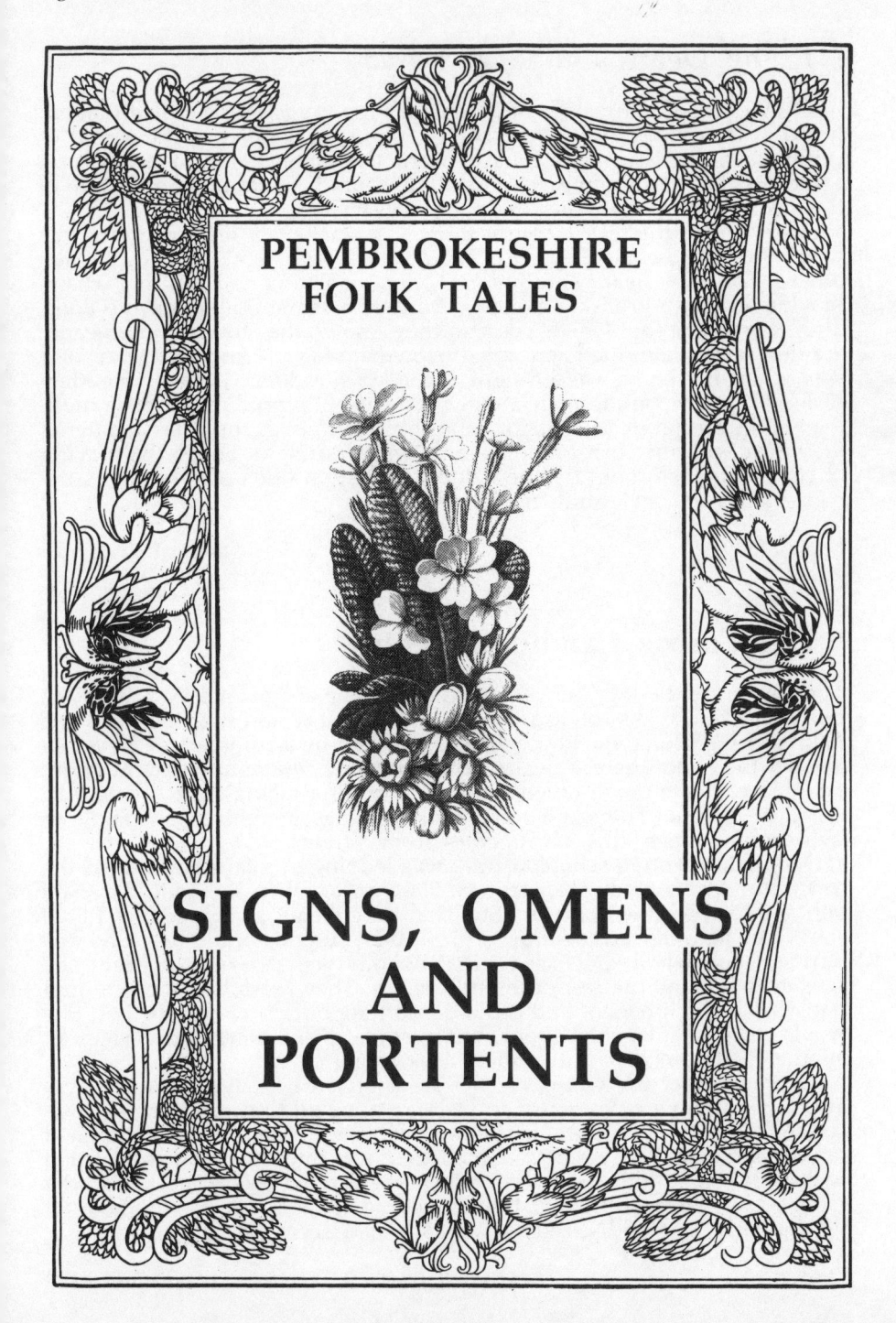

PEMBROKESHIRE FOLK TALES

SIGNS, OMENS AND PORTENTS

6.1 The Death Omen at Solva

In the Welsh-speaking areas of Pembrokeshire the *tolaeth* is a death omen, heard in the sound of a tolling bell or (more commonly) in the sound of coffin-making. Many people have heard the omen before a death, and carpenters have heard in precise detail the sounds of coffin manufacture in their workshops when they have been elsewhere.

One story of the *tolaeth* comes from Solva, where a fisherman and his wife were disturbed as they lay in bed on successive nights by eerie sounds downstairs. They heard shuffling feet, doors opening and shutting, chairs moving and men grunting as heavy burdens were set down on the floor. They were very frightened, because they knew what the sounds meant.

A few weeks later their son was drowned at sea. The first they knew of it was when his body was brought home on a ladder. With horror they realised that the sounds associated with the event reproduced exactly those they had heard at dead of night - the shuffling feet as the bearers entered the house with the corpse, the opening and shutting of doors, the moving of chairs to make room for the ladder, and the sounds of exertion as the men placed the makeshift bier on the floor.

Date : c 1850 ? *Source : Roberts p.25*

6.2 A Corpse Candle at Tenby

The corpse candle (*canwyll gorff*) was said to be a sign, particularly in the diocese of St David's, of a forthcoming death. It would take the form of a light passing along the route to be followed by a funeral, or hovering around the spot where a death would occur or where an accident might take place. If the death omen took the form of a falling light it would be called a *tanwedd*. There are records of sightings of the corpse candle in quite recent times; this story comes from Tenby.

One night a young schoolmistress was lodging in a farmhouse near the town. She was lying awake in the pitch darkness when she noticed a small light appear near the doorway. She later described it as being "like a little star". The light moved towards her bed, then stopped at her feet. She was terrified, and when she realised that nobody was carrying the light she screamed, waking the rest of the household. They ran to her room to find out what had happened, and could do nothing but try to console her. She would not remain in the room, but eventually she went off to sleep in another bedroom and the incident was forgotten.

Six weeks later the young teacher went off on holiday. While she was away the farmer's wife, who had been a strong and healthy woman, was suddenly taken ill. Although she was expected to recover she declined rapidly and died. The young schoolmistress was informed, and she hurried back just in time for the funeral. When she arrived she was taken to the room which she had previously occupied; and there she saw the body of the farmer's wife laid exactly where she had seen the corpse candle.

Date : c 1880 *Sources : Roberts p.32, Davies p.205, Radford p.142*

6.3 A Corpse Candle in Cwm Gwaun

In the early 1800s Mr Morris Griffiths was first a schoolmaster and then minister of Jabez Baptist Chapel at Pontfaen in the Gwaun Valley. One night he was returning home from Tredafydd when he saw a large red light over a section of the roadway not far from Llanychllwydog Church. He had heard about corpse candles, and assumed that this must be one, so being an educated and inquisitive man he watched with great interest to see what might happen next.

The *canwyll gorff* stood still over exactly the same spot on the road for about a quarter of an hour, and then, still as bright as ever, it moved into the church. Later it came out again and hovered over a spot in the churchyard. Then it disappeared.

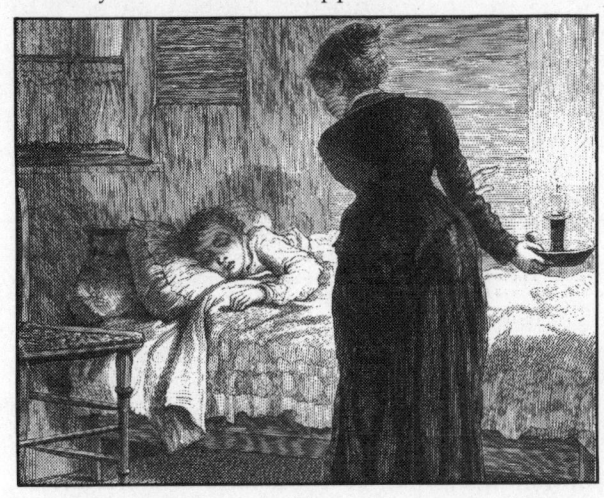

Next day, one of his pupils, the son of a Mr Higgon of Pontfaen, took to his bed with a mysterious illness.

A few days later, while Mr Griffiths was in school with the children, he heard a great noise overhead, and thought that the school roof was collapsing. He ran outside to investigate, but saw nothing.

Next day, one of his pupils, the son of a Mr Higgon of Pontfaen, took to his bed with a mysterious illness. A few days later the little boy died. When the carpenter came to fetch the boards for the coffin he had to climb up into the attic to fetch them, and while handling them he made a noise just like that which the schoolmaster had heard in school. Before the funeral took place there was a spell of very heavy rainfall, but the event went off more or less as planned. However, when the funeral procession was making its way to the church the roadway was flooded, and the passage of the coffin and mourners was delayed for some time while those who had boots assisted others across the flooded area. This episode took a quarter of an hour, and occurred exactly where Mr Griffiths had observed the light hovering. Then the procession went into the church, and later the boy was buried in exactly that part of the churchyard indicated by the corpse candle ten days before.

Date : c 1810 ?   Sources : Sikes p.244, W. Howells, p.61

6.4 The Mark of Cain

The village of Herbranston, not far from Milford Haven, has the unusual distinction that in two World Wars all of the local men who saw active service returned safely - 24 in the First World War and 43 in the Second. It is said that a guardian angel has watched over the parish for centuries, and there is a tomb in St Mary's Church supposed to be that of a crusader who miraculously survived the Holy Wars.

But one soldier who died violently is buried in the churchyard. In 1875 Lieutenant Phillip Walker of the Royal Artillery was stationed in nearby South Hook Fort. On 28th May, after a battalion dinner, there was a great deal of drinking and revelry. A bitter quarrel developed between Lieutenant Walker and a fellow officer, and as they struggled in a drunken rage the young man was stabbed to death. The murder trial caused quite a stir in the county, and the local people were outraged when the accused officer was acquitted. Phillip Walker, aged only 26, was buried behind the church of St Mary the Virgin, and his marble tombstone can still be seen.

Several months after the burial a strange manifestation was observed in the churchyard. Somebody noticed that following the installation of the headstone a clear outline of a hand and a dagger had appeared. Many attempts were made to wash it away, but it remained indelible. The old people of the village will still tell you that it is a sign of divine retribution - the mark of Cain.

Date : 1875 *Source : Radford p.51*

6.5 Phantom Funeral at Penally

There are many tales in Pembrokeshire concerning fetches or phantom funerals which were always held to be portents of real events. In Welsh the word *toili* is used for a phantom funeral. One such tale concerns Holloway Farm near Penally. On a winter's evening an employee of the Vicar of Penally saw a large phantom funeral procession near Holloway Farm, and he recognized several neighbours among the mourners. The Vicar laughed at the man when told about this, and showed even greater scepticism when told that the phantom funeral had left the road, passing over a hedge bank into an adjacent field and then returning to the road a hundred yards or so further along. The Vicar continued to express his doubts, adding "If this has indeed happened, you must surely be able to show me the place, since the hedge will be all trampled down." So the man took the Vicar to the place, but there was no sign of any disturbance.

Shortly after this there was a spell of severe weather, with heavy snowfall, during which Mr Williams, the tenant of Holloway Farm, died. On its way to the church the funeral party found the lane blocked by snow, and the coffin was carried over the hedge bank at precisely the spot crossed by the phantom funeral some days earlier. All the mourners followed, and the procession walked along the edge of the field, eventually returning to the lane in precisely the spot foreseen in the "fetch funeral".

Date : c 1850 *Source : Roberts p.31*

6.6 Disaster at Landshipping

In the year 1844 the Garden Pit colliery at Landshipping was the largest colliery in Pembrokeshire, employing 163 people. Many of the workforce, as was usual at that time on the Pembrokeshire Coalfield, were women, and there were also many boys under 14 years of age working at the coalface and hauling trucks on the underground tramways. The pit was located very close to Landshipping Quay; the main shaft was 65 yards deep, and the workings ran far out under the tidal estuary of the Daugleddau. Conditions in the pit were primitive and the owner, Hugh Owen, and his colliery management were renowned as hard taskmasters.

On 13th February 1844 the workers at the coalface were seriously worried - and not just because it was the thirteenth day of the month. The workings were shallow, and had been extended very close to the river bed, and that evening the men noticed with alarm that they could hear the sound of oars above them as the lighter vessels were rowed downstream on the high tide. A collier who was dumb noticed water leaking into the workings beneath the river and gesticulated to the foreman that the mine was in a dangerous condition. No action was taken, so he tried to pass on his message by scratching with a stone on the timber pit-props. The men expressed their concern to the management, since they knew that tomorrow there would be a Spring tide which would bring a huge weight of water to bear over the colliery workings. The manager would have none of it, and forced the next shift to go underground as usual.

Next day, St Valentine's Day, as the high tide surged up the river towards Picton Point, the roof of the workings collapsed and the Garden Pit was flooded by a catastrophic rush of water. The men and boys working underground had no hope of escape. Forty of them were killed, and there are still people living locally who believe that the real figure was seventy to eighty, with the official figure falsified to cover the fact that many of those lost were children supposedly too young to be at work in the pit.

After the disaster a mysterious notice, written in Latin, appeared on the headgear of the Garden Pit. It had to be examined by the vicar, who was the only person locally who understood Latin, and he translated it to the effect that the coal industry at Landshipping would never prosper again. The management swiftly removed the notice, but the next night it appeared again. The miners believed that a curse had been placed upon the Landshipping coal industry; and sure enough, no subsequent attempts at coal mining proved to be successful in the district either under the Owen family or their successors.

Date : 1844   Source : Price p.233

6.7 Phantom Funeral at Cilgwyn

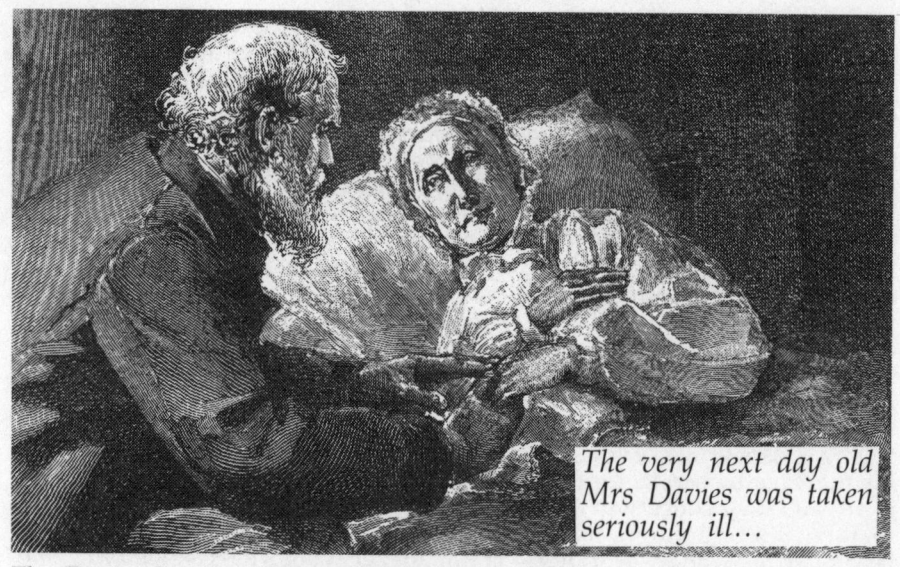

The very next day old Mrs Davies was taken seriously ill...

The Davies family of Felin Cilgwyn were reputed to have had the gift of second sight, and around the year 1905 Miss Martha Davies told how her mother had seen the phantom of her own funeral before she died.

The old lady was out walking down the lane from Caersalem Chapel to Felin Cilgwyn one night when she was terrified by a phantom funeral procession coming up the hill towards her. Although the lane is very narrow at that point, the funeral passed her by, and she noticed that the Vicar of Pontfaen, Rev Jenkin Evans, was walking behind the procession. This was unusual, for there would normally be no reason for a minister of the Church in Wales to be attending a funeral in the Baptist Chapel of Caersalem. When Mrs Davies returned home, greatly shaken by the episode, she described the Vicar's clothes in detail, and made special mention of his hat.

The very next day old Mrs Davies was taken seriously ill, and before long she was dead. Everybody in the neighbourhood believed that she had seen an apparition of her own funeral. She belonged to Caersalem Chapel herself, and so that is where the family arranged for the funeral to be held.

Her daughter Martha was at that time a maidservant at Pontfaen Vicarage, and the Vicar felt it his duty to accompany the girl to the funeral. He drove her from Pontfaen in his carriage, and left the pony and trap at the Pen-y-Bont inn, just up the road, since there was very little room at Felin Cilgwyn. He accompanied Martha to the house of mourning on foot, and later followed the funeral procession along the lane to Caersalem Chapel, again on foot. Martha later said that the scene - even down to the Vicar's clothes and hat - was exactly as her mother had described from her vision a few days before her death.

Date : c 1900 *Source : Davies p.198*

6.8 Phantom Funeral at Llanychaer

This story of a *Toili* or Phantom Funeral was told to the Rev J Ceredig Davies by the person who saw it, only four weeks after the event. At the time the young man involved was so terrified by the memory that he still refused to go out at night.

During the month of October 1905 a young porter who worked for the GWR near Cardiff came home ill to Llanychaer, in the Gwaun Valley. His condition caused great concern in the family. Dafydd, a young friend of his who lived nearby, sat up with him all night to keep him company; but at about 3 am the patient became so poorly that the lad decided to fetch his father, who lived in a small cottage down the road.

As soon as Dafydd set foot outside the door he was astonished to find that he was in the midst of a large crowd of people. He noticed a coffin resting on two chairs, ready to be placed on a bier, and concluded that this must be a funeral party ready to move off to the church. When Dafydd attempted to walk down the road towards the cottage where his friend's father lived, the procession moved in the same direction, so he found himself a part of the crowd. He walked in the midst of the throng for almost a hundred yards, and managed to extract himself when he reached the old man's front door. He hammered on the door, almost passing out from the shock of what he had experienced.

Three days later the young railway porter died, and on the day of the funeral all was exactly as Dafydd had foreseen, with the coffin resting on the two chairs, the throng of people assembled outside the house, and the procession moving off down the road past the front door of the father's cottage.

Date : 1905
Sources : Davies p.193, Roberts p.21

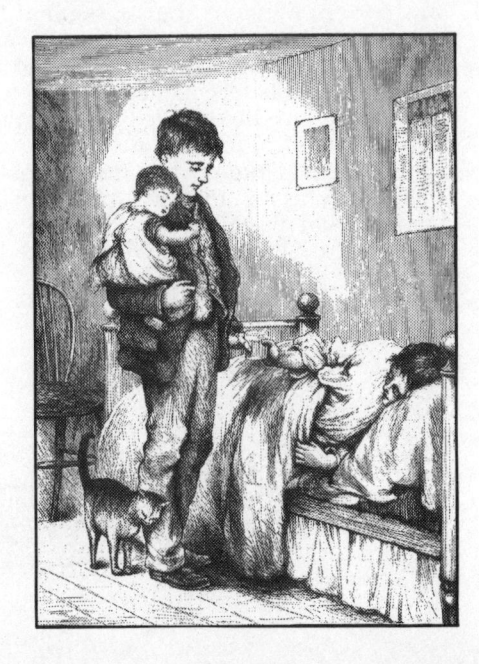

His condition caused great concern in the family......

6.9 The Unfaithful Wife of William the Fleming

Around the middle of the twelfth century, in the time of Giraldus Cambrensis, there were many Flemish immigrants in Pembrokeshire. Most settled in the Haverfordwest area. They were renowned for their powers of divination, and used for this purpose the right shoulder-blades of rams which had been boiled (not roasted) and stripped of all flesh.

One William Mangunel was well known for his special powers, as was his young wife, who was very much younger than him. But his wife was unfaithful, and William knew that the child she was carrying was not his but that of his own grandson. He was sorely troubled by this incestuous relationship, and determined to gain an admission from his wife as to her wicked ways. One day he took a ram from his flock, and killed it. Two days later, pretending that it was gift from a neighbour, he presented the carcass to his wife and suggested that it should be prepared for supper that very same evening. She sent it down to the cook to be prepared, and in due course they sat down at the dinner table and were served with fine steaming portions of boiled mutton and fresh vegetables.

Before they started to eat the meat, William nonchalantly passed his wife the right shoulder-blade of the animal, boiled according to the recipe and now carefully cleaned. She took the bone and examined it minutely, fingering the cracks and all its secret markings. Her study of the prophetic bone continued for some little time, and then with a smile she threw it onto the table. William appeared unconcerned, but pressed her as to the cause of her amusement. Without thinking about what she was saying, she laughed "Husband, the man from whose flock this ram was taken has a wife who has broken the marriage vows. What is more," she continued, "at this very moment she is pregnant from commerce with his grandson."

Too late she realised that the ram had not come from a neighbour's flock but from their own, and that she had been trapped by her husband into a confession. William was not angry but downcast, for, as he said, it was he who had to face the public humiliation. As for the unfaithful wife, she was covered with confusion and then overcome with remorse. She blushed bright red and then went deadly pale. And then she began to cry.

Unfortunately Giraldus Cambrensis, who recounted this tale, did not divulge what happened in the end to the husband, or the wife, or the grandson, or the innocent newborn baby.

Date : c 1150   *Source : Giraldus p.146*

PEMBROKESHIRE FOLK TALES

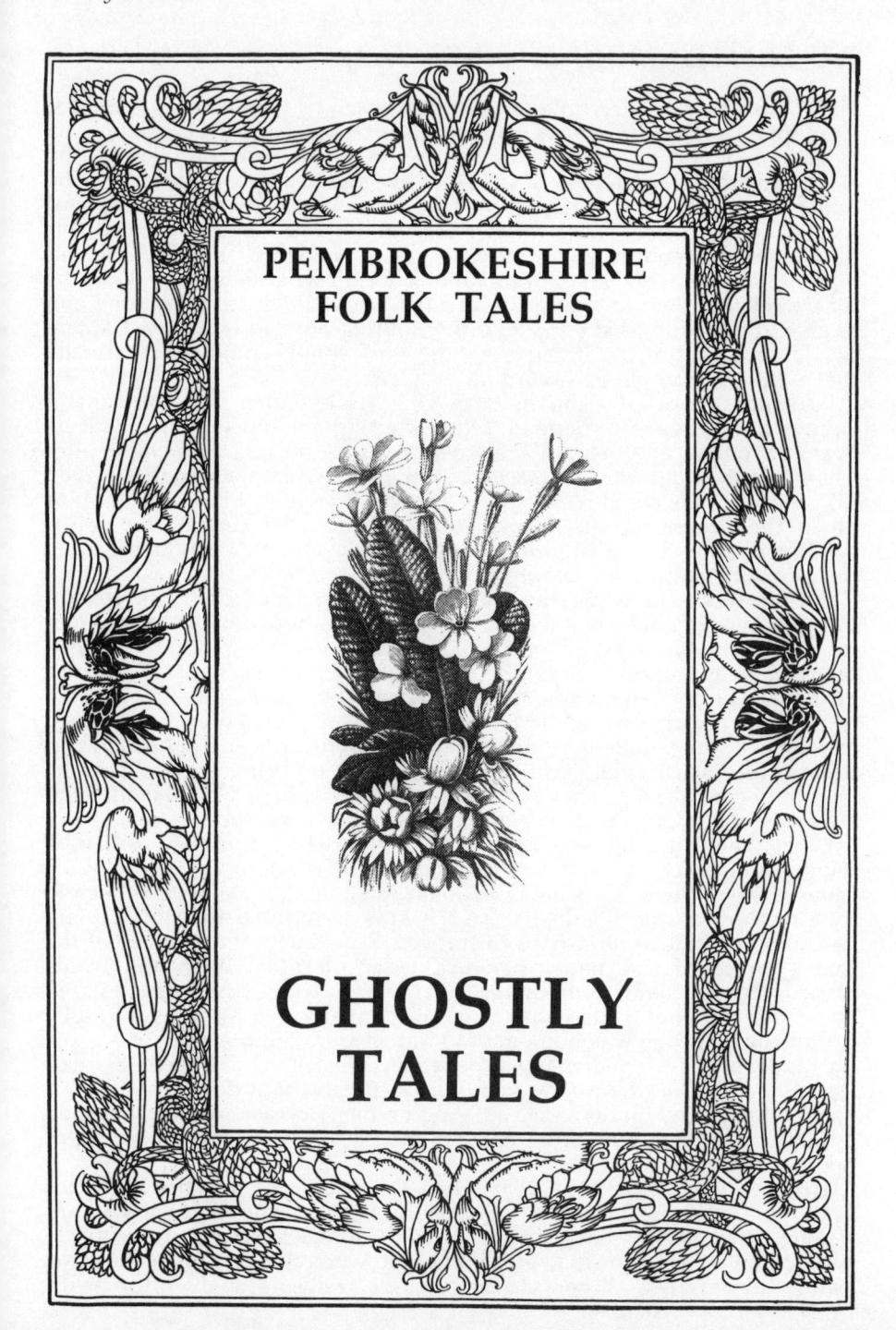

GHOSTLY TALES

7.1 The Haunting of HMS "Asp"

HMS **Asp** was a small paddle steamer purchased by the Navy and based at Pembroke Dockyard for surveying work. In 1850 a Captain Alldridge took command of the vessel, and as he was being shown round it by the Dockyard Superintendent he was informed that the ship was haunted. The Superintendent said that he doubted if he could get any of the Dockyard men to work in her, such was her reputation. The Captain greeted this news with a sceptical smile; but the vessel needed to be repaired and refitted, and the work was put in hand. The shipwrights worked on board for a week; but then they came as a body to the Captain and implored him to give up the ship as she would bring nothing but bad luck. The Captain would not hear of it and insisted that the work should continue. Eventually the re-fit was completed according to plan.

But once the ship began its surveying work under the new captain strange things began to happen. Often the Captain and the other officers heard banging, clattering and strange inexplicable noises in the empty after cabin, which could only be reached by the companion ladder that served his cabin also. He could see from his own cabin anyone who climbed up or down the ladder on the way to or from the after cabin. The noises continued, and were most prominent on quiet evenings when he sat alone in his cabin reading by lamplight.

On one occasion when the ship was visiting Queensferry in Ireland Captain Alldridge returned on board one night to hear noises coming from his own cabin. He thought he had caught the ghost at last, and burst open the door, only to find that all was just as normal inside, with no ghost to be seen. Shortly afterwards, the Quartermaster came in with news of trouble on board. The night lookout had seen the figure of a woman standing on the paddle-box and pointing heavenward. The poor man had been so terrified that he fled from his post; and on being ordered back he went into convulsions. The result was that the Captain, who was made of sterner stuff, angrily had to complete the watch himself.

Later, when the ship was back in the Milford Haven waterway, it was lying peacefully at anchor at Lawrenny one Sunday afternoon. The steward came to the Captain in a state of extreme agitation, having been spoken to by a mysterious disembodied voice. He was so terrified that the Captain had to allow him to go ashore to recover. Subsequently a number of the sailors on board also had experiences which terrified them and which caused them to request discharge. On being refused, the men deserted ship, and the ship's surveying work was greatly disrupted as a result.

Captain Alldridge was not a man to retreat from the presence of a ghost on his ship but he had many experiences himself which made his hair stand on end. Once he was woken up in a cold sweat at dead of night by a hand being placed on his forehead. And on many occasions he was woken by drawers in his cabin being opened and closed, and by the banging of his wash-stand top.

Things came to a head in 1857 when the vessel put into the Dockyard again for repairs. On the first night in harbour the dockyard sentry reported that he had seen the figure of a woman climbing up onto the paddle-box, where she stood and pointed towards the sky. Then she came ashore towards him. When challenged, she walked straight through his musket, upon which he dropped it and fled in disarray to the guard-house. A second sentry witnessed the whole episode and himself fired at the apparition, with no effect. And a third sentry saw the figure enter the old Pater Churchyard, where it mounted a grave and disappeared from sight. All the guards in the Dockyard were so scared by the news of this event that the guard had to be doubled.

However, the departure of the ghost from the ship to the Churchyard signalled the end of the haunting, and the unhappy woman was never seen again. In seeking an explanation for the strange events on board his ship, Captain Alldridge later discovered that prior to being commissioned by the Navy, HMS **Asp** had been an Irish packet boat. After one trip, a stewardess had discovered the body of a beautiful girl in the aft cabin, where she had travelled as a passenger. Her throat had been cut, and nothing was ever discovered about her or about the perpetrator of the crime.

Date : 1850   *Sources : Roberts p.27, Davies p.169*

7.2 David of the Charnel-House

In the early 1800s there was a strange fellow called David who lived in the village of Pill (near Milford). He was assumed to be mad, for he was quite fearless, and took to sleeping every night in the charnel-house near the church, among the piles of human bones and skulls.

One day the local lads determined to give David a fright, and a few of them dressed up in white sheets and crept up to the charnel-house at dead of night. They then proceeded to make eerie noises, moving back and forth in front of the charnel-house door and pretending to be ghosts. However, they got more than they bargained for. Far from making his hair stand on end, the lads caused David to wake up in a furious temper. And knowing precisely what **real** ghosts were like, he chased off the intruders, shouting "O you are devils sure enough, and I am David of Pill, so here's what you get!" And with that he started throwing stones at the lads in white, causing them to suffer from an assortment of cuts and bruises as they fled in disarray.

David continued to sleep in the charnel-house for several weeks after this, but one night he encountered something far more evil than a normal ghost, and fled in terror from his house of rest. After that, he returned home, and for the rest of his life refused ever to go out again after dark. His family and friends were firmly of the opinion that on the fateful night he had encountered an extremely unpleasant supernatural being in the dark shadows among the piles of white bones.

Date : c 1750 ?   *Source : Howells, W. p.20*

7.3 The Bush House Ghosts

Bush House, not far from Pembroke, has long had the reputation of being one of the most haunted houses in Pembrokeshire. It was once the home of the Meyrick family, one of whom was old John Meyrick, the Chief Justice of South Wales and a thorough scoundrel to boot. The locals were convinced that he was rewarded for his wicked ways by being carried off by the Devil, for his body seems to have disappeared in mysterious circumstances. At any rate his ghost, in the form of a dignified old gentleman, has often been encountered inside the house during the hours of darkness.

In 1955 there were a number of strange occurrences when three workmen from Manchester were employed on conversion work at Bush House. For a while the men slept in one of the rooms in the house, but no sooner had they moved in than they noticed a cold heavy atmosphere there during the hours of darkness. The Tilley lamp which they used in the room behaved in a very erratic way; there were bangings and rattling noises from the doors and walls; and the youngest of the workmen felt sharp tuggings on the overcoat which he used as a bed-cover. The three were so frightened that they bolted one of the doors into the room and closed the other one with battens and nails. But still the noises and the tugging on the bedclothes continued.

On the second night the men refused to sleep in the same room and moved instead to a room on the top floor of the house. From the window of this room they observed, glowing in the moonlight, the figure of a lady dressed in a crinoline gown walking back and forth on the path outside. The men fled from the house in the middle of the night and refused to sleep there again.

On another occasion, after Bush House became a part of Bush School, a night watchman was doing his rounds outside the old building at 2 am when he suddenly encountered an elderly gentleman of medium build wearing breeches, leggings and an old shooting jacket. Under his arm he carried a double-barrelled sporting gun, and by his side were three dogs. The watchman spoke to the figure, first in English and then in Welsh, but he received no reply, and then the ghostly sportsman and his dogs walked off and disappeared into a small pond. The "old-fashioned" gentleman with his three dogs has also been seen by many other people from the area over the years.

One explanation of the phantom sportsman and the lady in the crinoline gown can be found in nineteenth-century local history. Apparently a gentleman of Bush House was out shooting one day with his dogs in the grounds, while his wife travelled into Pater (the old name for Pembroke Dock) in her coach. When she returned her husband met the coach on the way home, and as she opened the door to speak to him, the gun went off by accident. The lady was mortally wounded, and the poor man never recovered from the tragedy.

Date : 1955   Source : Underwood p.153

7.4 Wake Night at Dolrannog

On the south-facing slope of Carningli, not far from Newport, there is a farm called Dolrannog Isaf. Here, towards the end of the eighteenth century, an eerie event occurred which has subsequently become a part of local folk-lore.

A wicked old farmer, who had made no secret of his dislike for all matters religious, had died and was laid out in his coffin. The *gwylnos* or wake night went on as normal, with many people calling to pay their last respects and with much merriment among family and friends. Candles were lit in the room where the body lay in its open coffin. As peace descended on the house in the early hours a few of the male members of the family maintained their vigil in the room next door.

Suddenly the relatives were startled to hear the sound of horses' hooves approaching at a gallop. They heard the horses stop outside the front door, but before they could investigate the house was plunged into darkness as all the candles were simultaneously extinguished. They heard the sound of heavy footsteps outside; then the front door was opened and the footsteps came into the house. They were all frozen with fear; nobody spoke and nobody moved. But they all felt and heard the invisible intruders go past them into the room where the corpse lay in its open coffin. Then the intruders went out again. The heavy footsteps reached the front door, which was then closed. All those present heard the sound of the horses being mounted again, and then off they went at a gallop into the distance. At last, all was silent again.

At first everybody was too frightened to investigate. But then somebody managed to relight the candles, and the feeling of terror began to subside. Cautiously, the men entered the room where the body had been laid, only to find that the coffin was empty. In spite of a frantic search the body was never found, and it was concluded by the family and neighbours that the Devil had come to claim his own. The coffin was filled with stones and later buried in Cilgwyn graveyard, with a minimum of religious ceremony, just for the sake of appearances.

Date : c 1790 ?   Sources : Roberts p.18, Davies p.44, Radford p.154, Rhys p.73

7.5 The Vicar and the Headless Lady

Stackpole Court was one of the grandest houses in Pembrokeshire, having been built by the Earl of Cawdor at the end of the eighteenth century. The house, which had 300 rooms, became one of the busiest centres of social life for the local gentry; but by the year 1911 the estate had fallen on hard times, and in 1962 the mansion was demolished. Naturally enough, the old house had its share of ghosts.

In the latter part of the last century one of the ghosts of Stackpole Court was known locally as "Lady Mathias". She was headless, and was often seen riding by in her carriage, accompanied by a headless coachman and drawn by two headless horses. The phantom journeys were always made between Tenby and Sampson Cross, via Stackpole Court. Many attempts were made to rid the area of this headless old lady, but no exorcism was successful until the Vicar of St Petrox doomed her to empty Bosherston Lily Ponds with a cockle-shell as a ladle. She must have found this task somewhat daunting, and drove off into the ether, never to be seen again.

Date : c 1880 ? *Sources : Fenton p.232, Davies p.191*

7.6 Mr Warlow and the Phantom Boat

Around the year 1800, when the town of Milford was young, a wealthy wine merchant called John Warlow lived in Castle Hall. This magnificent mansion looked down on the shore of Castle Pill to the east of the town, and Mr Warlow made a habit of taking walks along the banks of the creek.

One fine summer's night he was walking home along the beach and enjoying the bright moonlight. Suddenly he heard the sound of a boat coming up the creek, which surprised him since the tide was out and the mudbanks were exposed. He could see no sign of a boat. The sounds continued, coming inexorably towards him. He heard the measured dip of oars in the water, the creaking of the rowlocks and the murmur of the bow wave. Presently he heard the sound of the keel scraping on the gravelly beach by the side of the old quay wall, and then the sound of heavy feet on the steps of the quay. Still he saw nothing.

Greatly alarmed by this strange occurrence, Mr Warlow hurried back up the hill to Castle Hall, and related the incident to his family. He told of the sounds he had heard, and also described the strange stillness which had surrounded him, as if all of the normal noises of a summer's night had been blotted out as long as the sounds of the phantom boat continued.

A few days later an East Indiaman anchored off shore. While it was there the mate died on board, and when the tide was sufficiently high his body in its coffin was brought ashore by rowing boat and landed in Castle Pill. The sailors beached their boat adjacent to the old quay and carried the coffin up the steps. Mr Warlow witnessed this event, and he observed that all of the sounds associated with it were exactly as he had heard them during his eerie experience in the moonlight.

Date : c 1800 *Source : Underwood p.121*

7.7 Goblins on Presely

In the Presely Hills there are many stories of encounters with ancient, awful beings, and there are many who believe that elemental forces still reign supreme among the rolling bleak moorlands and jagged rocks.

Not long ago a local man who had been a boxer in his younger days was walking alone near Foelfeddau, which is Welsh for "the bare hill with the graves". He was a big man, very fit and seemingly afraid of nothing in this world and probably little in the next. He was alone and utterly content, and had been walking for several hours in the quiet of the day, listening to skylarks above and other moorland birds around him.

Suddenly, as though a curtain had fallen, all about him changed completely and he felt the raw edge of fear. He felt that he was in the presence of the unknown. He looked about him. Everything looked the same, but now there were no sounds - no birdsong, no rustling of the breeze in the grass, no bleating of sheep. This was "The Presely Silence", which others have felt in the past and others will feel in the future. He stood still, feeling danger in the air and waiting for something to happen. He became aware that evil, invisible eyes were upon him. He swung round, but there was nothing there. A low laugh came from alongside him, as if he was being taunted by a *bwgan* or goblin. He turned again, but still could see nothing. He began to feel giddy and he sat down on the turf, closed his eyes and put his hands to his head. When he opened his eyes again he saw a group of small, hairy men, quite naked, carrying heavy clubs. They were walking towards him, muttering and laughing among themselves. They paid no attention to him, but came closer and closer and closer. He tried to get to his feet and found to his horror that he was held in a vice-like grip by some force he could not explain. He had always been a strong man but he found that he was quite powerless to move. With mounting horror he watched the approach of the small hairy men. Then he could contain himself no longer. He screamed with terror, closing his eyes as he did so.

When he opened his eyes again all was normal. The skylarks were singing, and he could hear the bleating of lambs in the distance. There was no sign of anyone - the goblins had disappeared without trace. Scrambling to his feet, our friend rushed away from the accursed spot. Afterwards, in relating the story, he said that he has tried to convince himself that it was all a bad dream. But he said that wild horses would never drag him to that place again.

Date : c 1965   Source : Underwood p.175

7.8 The Monkton Nun

When the Rev Tudor Evans lived with his family in Monkton Old Hall, not far from Pembroke Castle, he told a newspaper reporter about a series of very strange events.

On many occasions the Vicar was disturbed by heavy knocking on his bedroom door at precisely 4 am. He would get out of bed to see who was there, but as soon as his foot touched the floor the knocking would cease. And when he opened the door there was never anything to be seen. There was also a room in the house which the family dog steadfastly refused to enter, although it happily wandered about in every other room. Even when urged to enter the room the animal refused to budge. One day the Vicar's daughter saw a glow of light coming from the room when she was on the landing outside, and when she opened the door she saw quite distinctly the outline of the head and shoulders of a cowled figure, apparently leaning out of the window and waving.

After this the room came to be known as the "haunted room", and on one occasion a friend of the family slept there. Afterwards he related how he had heard the rustling of long garments around the bed all through the night. On several occasions he tried to light the candle at the bedside in order to investigate the source of the sound, but each time the candle was immediately and mysteriously snuffed out.

The mystery of the haunting at Monkton was solved later when during repair work in the Church of St Nicholas, Monkton, the remains of a kneeling woman were found bricked up inside a wall in the priest's room. It was later explained that there was an ancient Benedictine priory attached to the church, and the Rev Evans speculated that the body was that of a nun who had committed some sin which required penance. He believed that the haunting of the Old Hall was the result of this sin which had kept the nun's spirit "earthbound".

Date : 1934   *Source : Underwood p.124*

7.9 A Lady in White at Manorbier Castle

. . . he had jumped across the stream in a state of panic before passing out.

Manorbier Castle was the childhood home of Giraldus Cambrensis, and it has seen life and death over a period of 800 years. One of the three ghosts said to inhabit the castle is a lady in white, who figured in a strange episode during the First World War. At the time a group of soldiers were on duty in the castle, having been detailed to keep a constant watch on the coast for fear of enemy action. At night the soldiers went on guard two by two. One night one of the two guards fell ill, so the sergeant took him off to the doctor and promised his colleague that he would send a replacement as soon as possible. At last the replacement soldier arrived, but he could find no trace of the lone watchman. He searched everywhere, first inside the castle and then in the village outside. At last he found him lying unconscious on the village green, with his rifle abandoned on the other side of the stream. Clearly he had jumped across the stream in a state of panic before passing out.

When the soldier came round he related that he had seen a lady in white coming towards him. He had challenged her, but still she came on, so at last he had fired at her. The bullet had passed clean through her, upon which she disappeared from sight. Alone among the dark shadows of the castle, the poor man had been so terrified that he had fled towards the village as fast as his legs could carry him.

Date : c 1915   Source : Pembs Mag 24

7.10 The Battle in the Sky

Mynydd Morfil is one of the lower foothills of Presely, not far from Puncheston and Pontfaen. The area round about is one of bleak windswept moorlands, with few farms and no proper clusters of settlement.

One night in 1853 Mr John Meyler of Cilciffeth was walking home from Morfil. As he passed Penterfin he was distracted by a vision of armies in the sky. There were two armies, clearly visible overhead, locked in a life-or-death struggle for supremacy. As he walked on he watched the spectral armies become larger and larger, till at last there were thousands of warriors, many on horseback, galloping at each other, with horses and men falling under the assault of enemy swords, spears and battle-axes. Mr Meyler was so terrified by the vision that he called at Penbanc, where Mr James Morris lived. Mr Morris came outside and together the two men watched the battle, which continued for a further two hours. Then the vision disappeared and Mr Meyler continued on his way.

There are a number of records of spectral armies in the sky, and this is not the only one from the vicinity of Mynydd Morfil (see also 7.11).

It has been suggested that this vision was a premonition of the Crimean War which started about six months later. However, it is more likely that Mr Meyler and Mr Morris were watching a "ghostly replay" of the Battle of Mynydd Carn, a terrible encounter which took place around the year 1081 between the armies of Gruffydd ap Cynan and Rhys ap Tewdwr on the one side and Trahaearn and Caradog on the other. This battle was crucial in the struggle for supremacy between the Welsh princes round about the time of the Norman invasion. At Mynydd Carn there was appalling loss of life; and the battle is well recorded in Welsh history. But the site has never been found. One of the most educated guesses is that the battle took place in the wild hills around Morfil and Castlebythe.

Date : 1853   Sources : Roberts p.18, Warner p.59, Radford p.150, Davies p.273, Lewis p.101.

7.11 The Phantom Armies of Mynydd Morfil

Once upon a time there was a whitewashed farmhouse on the slopes of Mynydd Morfil, overlooking the woodland of Ty-rhyg. The farmhouse was inhabited by a farmer, his wife, and two young sons. The land was rough and stony, and they made their living as shepherds, tending their flocks on the wild windswept moorlands of Mynydd Morfil and Pen Palis.

One evening the farmer was out on the hills with the two boys when the strangest thing happened. The sun was setting over Mynydd Cilciffeth and to the east cumulus clouds were piled up over the summit of Foel Eryr. A golden path seemed to be laid across the sky by shafts of light from the setting sun. Suddenly the clouds darkened and a gust of wind disturbed the silence. Then a distant sound like thunder rolled over the hills. The shepherd thought it was thunder, but then he realised that he was hearing the sound of galloping horses' hooves - thousands of them, thundering across the sky and echoing through the darkening valleys and hills.

He could hardly believe his eyes when he looked to the north-east and saw that a battalion of foot-soldiers was marching over the horizon, seeming to materialize from the base of the clouds which now masked the summit of Foel Eryr. He could see their shields, armour and spears glinting and gleaming in the golden rays of the setting sun. He could hear a drumbeat as the soldiers marched steadily on, and then he saw the mounted soldiers also, holding back their horses as the army advanced.

The shepherd's two sons were looking in the opposite direction, transfixed by what they saw. "Look, father!" they shouted. "Look at Mynydd Cilciffeth!" The shepherd turned and he too saw that over the top of that bleak moorland summit came another army, rushing at full speed towards the foe. Again there were foot-soldiers and horsemen; again their weapons and armour flashed as they came out of the setting sun. The watchers felt their blood run cold as they heard the whine of a thousand flighted arrows, and then the screams and yells of the soldiers as the two armies joined in battle.

As the silver-edged clouds raced overhead the shepherd and his son saw flails, swords and battle-axes used to terrible effect. Metal clashed with metal. Horses reared up and fell, mortally wounded. Men engaged with one another in bloody conflict. Shields and helmets were battered or split. Long spears and darts arched through the air, and men screamed and shouted, some in triumph and others in agony. The battle was fierce and bloody, and lasted for more than an hour as darkness fell.

Then a huge flash of lightning split the sky as black thunder clouds closed in above Mynydd Morfil; and a torrential downpour swept across the hills, accompanied by daggers of lightning and deafening peals of thunder directly overhead. The shepherd and his sons had never experienced such a storm; they found shelter beneath a rocky crag, and there they remained for more than an hour. At last the rain stopped and the clouds cleared, and the three made their way homewards in bright moonlight beneath a velvet sky.

The storm was remembered for many years by others in the locality, but the shepherd and his two sons were the only people to see the phantom battle. They never forgot it, and the memory was passed down from generation to generation, persisting as a part of local folk-lore. In the meantime, the little whitewashed farm on the flank of Mynydd Morfil was abandoned and eventually reduced to a pile of stones almost lost in the heather moorland.

It can be no coincidence that both this story and the previous one (7.10) are set in the vicinity of Mynydd Morfil. But the stories are clearly not related, for they have different characters and different local details. This story reinforces our belief that the phantom battle was indeed that of "Mynydd Carn", and one little detail in particular is fascinating. In this story the army in the north-east appears to be the defending army, while the soldiers coming out of the setting sun appear to have been on the attack. From the old records this is precisely what happened at the Battle of Mynydd Carn; the defending army of Trahaearn and Caradog had come from Gwynedd (in other words from the north-east), whereas the army of Gruffydd and Rhys had landed at Porth-clais and marched for a full day towards the north-east from St David's. They were impatient for battle, and attacked without hesitation as soon as their scouts spotted the enemy at sunset. They may well have swooped down from the summit of Mynydd Cilciffeth with the sun at their backs, just as the shepherd and his sons observed centuries later. There is no way that these tactical details could have been known to the simple folk who lived on the farms near Morfil.

Date : c 1750 ?   Sources : T.P. Lewis, p.101, Radford p.150, H. Williams, p17.

7.12 A Haunting at Castlebythe

The remote hamlet of Castlebythe is located in the western foothills of Mynydd Presely, to the south of the lonely valley of Cwm Gwaun. It is an area of bleak open moorland, seldom visited by strangers and renowned for its ghostly happenings. This story is a classic one, involving a poltergeist and a teenage girl.

One evening around the year 1900, the family of Castlebythe Farm were seated around the fire in the flickering light of paraffin lamps when the silence was broken by a voice. It seemed to come from outside, but on investigation nobody could be found, and as the voice continued a chill of fear descended on the family. After a while silence returned, soon to be shattered by a clattering noise outside. Someone investigated, to discover that the big butter churn in the dairy was turning end-over-end with nobody near enough to turn the handle. There was a large stone rattling inside it, and it was only with the greatest difficulty that the men of the family managed to stop the churn to get it out.

Next night the whole episode was repeated, and so it continued night after night. Word of the haunting spread around the area, and some of the bolder neighbours came to hear the strange voice and see the turning butter churn for themselves. The spirit or *bwca* appeared quite harmless, but it was a nuisance nonetheless. At last, with the family greatly irritated by the activities of the mysterious intruder, some of the men decided to keep watch outside with a shotgun for protection. They hid close to the farm behind some big trees, and heard the voice but saw no movement. The next night they kept watch again. They heard the voice and thought they saw something move near the dairy, so they let fly with both barrels of the shotgun. There was a strange flare of light in the trees, but that was all. As the men trooped back inside, the farmer suddenly noticed that the one person apparently unaffected by all the commotion was Marie, the servant girl, who was sitting quietly in the corner as usual. He sensed that there must be some link between the girl and the eerie visitations, and next day he dismissed her from his service. After that, the strange voice was never heard again, and the butter churn remained quiet in the dairy.

Date : c 1900   *Source: Roberts p.19*

7.13 The Black Dog of Pant-y-Madog

Pant-y-Madog lies not far from Laugharne, and like many other places in West Wales it has a traditional guardian in the form of a fearsome phantom hound or *gwyllgi*. The black dog in this case is said to spring up from a deep flooded pit at the roadside. According to tradition this pit leads down directly to the underworld.

One of the sightings of the black dog involved a young girl called Rebecca Adams, who lived in a cottage near the castle at Laugharne. Her mother sent her into town one evening on an errand, telling her jokingly to beware of the ghostly hound of Pant-y-Madog. The girl set out upon her way, and was relieved to pass the roadside pit where the dog was said to reside; but then she was suddenly confronted by an enormous black hound with glowing red eyes, which showed its fangs and uttered a bloodcurdling growl. The dog bounded towards her, but then stopped in front of her, squatted on its haunches "and set up such a scream, so loud, so horrible, and so strong that she thought the earth moved under her." Later on, when the girl failed to return from her errand, her mother and a number of neighbours set out to look for her, and found her unconscious at the side of the road. She was quite unharmed, and later recounted her terrifying experience.

After this the *gwyllgi* was seen many times by lonely travellers who journeyed along the same road; but it appears that its bark was worse than its bite, for nobody was ever harmed by it.

Date : c 1800 ? Sources : Brooks p.63, Davies p.182, Sikes p.170

....*a number of neighbours set out to look for her, and found her unconscious at the side of the road.*

7.14 The Jolly Sailor and the Dog of Baal

Once upon a time there was a seafaring man "of pronounced rollicking habits" who lodged with his brother in Cwm (Lower Town, Fishguard) when on land. One night the jolly sailor was returning happily from Cefn-y-dre to the Cwm, when on reaching the bridge over the Gwaun River he had an unpleasant encounter with the great black Dog of Baal.

The infernal dog was of huge size, sooty black, with flaming red eyes as big as oysters. He had a chain around his neck, which crashed and rattled as he bounded towards the sailor. The poor man was paralysed with fear, and became quite convinced that the creature was going to seize him and carry him off for his sins to the very hot regions where Baal is said to dwell. As the dog rushed at him open-mouthed, with a muffled roar like the sound of distant breakers in a hurricane, the sailor man cried out to God for mercy and pardon, seeking instant salvation through the Sacred Name.

The Dog of Baal was about to sink his great fangs into the sailor's leg, but as soon as the name of God was uttered the creature sprang back, with a howl of rage that rang from the top of Pen Twr on the one side to Carn Mawr on the other side of the valley. Then, with a parting glare of fiendish fury, it leaped into the river and disappeared.

The intended victim, when he saw that the Cwm end of the bridge was now clear of the enemy, rushed to the front door of his brother's house and kicked and beat upon it in a panic. Then, when his brother opened it, he fell in a faint upon the threshold.

The sailor's brother and sister were much affected by this incident. As for the sailor himself, it is said that he actually went to church on the Sunday following his encounter with the infernal hound - something which was very much out of character.

One night the jolly sailor was returning happily from Cefn-y-dre to the Cwm....

Date : c 1850

Source : Rhys p.32

7.15 Mr Walter and the Phantom Dog

During the nineteenth century Mr David Walter was walking across a field called Cot Moor, in which there are two standing stones called the Devil's Nags. These stones were said to be haunted, but Mr Walter did not believe such things. Suddenly, without any visible sign of beast or man, he felt himself being lifted up in the air, upon which he was unceremoniously dumped on the other side of a hedge.

Next time he went for a walk across the field he took a strong fighting dog mastiff with him for protection, but as he approached the Devil's Nags he saw blocking his path the apparition of a dog more terrible than any he had ever seen. In vain he tried to set his mastiff onto the beast; but his dog crouched by his master's feet and refused to move. Mr Walter then picked up a heavy stone, thinking that this might frighten the hound. Immediately a circle of fire surrounded the animal, and in the bright light he could see the fearsome fangs and grinning teeth, and caught a glimpse of a white tip to the long tail. The dog then disappeared; but Mr Walter knew that he had seen one of the infernal dogs of hell.

Date : c 1800 ? *Sources : Davies p.181, Sykes p.170*

7.16 The Cwn Annwn at Laugharne

Not far from Laugharne Castle is the old cross-roads where the gallows were located in days gone by. Over the centuries many felons were hanged here, and the place was reputed to be haunted by the *Cwn Annwn* or Hounds of Hell. Sometimes they hunt in packs, as we know from the story of Pwll, but sometimes single dogs would be seen, and when they were abroad the people would bolt their doors and shutter their windows.

In the early years of the last century a fisherman was returning from the estuary, and it was getting dark as he made for his home in the town. The wind howled, and there was rain in the air. As he approached the cross-roads he became aware that something was watching him, and he heard a low growl behind him. Looking back, he saw a huge white hound crouching in the long grass. His hair stood on end, for the hound was quite unlike any he had ever seen before. As he watched, the spectral hound sprang towards him. The fisherman turned on his heel and ran towards the cross-roads, feeling the hot breath of the beast on the back of his neck. In his haste he stumbled and fell, and in a flash the great white hound was upon him, placing its huge front paws on his chest and pinning him to the ground.

The poor fisherman felt that his hour had come. "Duw a'm helpo!" (God help me!) he cried, as the animal prepared to sink its fangs into his arm. Suddenly the beast let out a frightful howl, and the fisherman saw the animal's figure grow fainter and fainter until it had disappeared altogether. Not waiting to see what had happened to it, the man picked himself up off the ground and ran all the way home, battered and bruised but otherwise none the worse for his adventure.

Date: c 1830 *Source: Radford p 158*

7.17 Broad Haven and the Aliens

During 1977 a number of very strange incidents brought the south-east corner of St Bride's Bay to national and even international attention. These incidents involved unidentified flying objects, strange beings and close encounters of various types, all well authenticated.

On 4th February 1977 children in the playground of Broad Haven CP School saw what they took to be a spacecraft landing in a nearby field. The children saw that the vehicle was silvery-yellow, and was cigar-shaped. It also had windows, and while they watched a figure with a helmet on came out of it, looking as if it had a "sort of camera". It was lunch-break, and unfortunately the headmaster ignored the pleas of the children to come and look at the object which had attracted their attention. Only 13 days later there was a second incident, this time witnessed by adults and in the same general area. A similar cigar-shaped object glided off with a humming noise, seen by the teacher and two canteen workers. More importantly, they also saw a figure climb out of the vehicle when it was on the ground.

On the evening of 13th March a 17-year-old lad from Pen-y-Cwm saw a glowing oval object in the sky near Hendre Bridge. He was also startled by an extremely large black dog which padded past him silently and which seemed to have come from the direction of the UFO. Later he walked past the perimeter fence of RAF Brawdy and encountered a large dome-shaped object, at least twenty feet high and 30-40 feet wide, with a faint glow around its edge. As he looked at it he noticed a tall figure coming towards him. It was dressed in a near-transparent suit, and had a strange head with fixed staring eyes. It kept on coming, so the lad took a swipe at it. He failed to connect, but he was so terrified that he ran all the way home.

A number of strange events were centred on Ripperston Farm. On 12th April the farmer's wife and children were followed in their car by a strange light, which eventually caused the vehicle to suffer from a complete electrical failure. On 24th April the whole family saw a huge space-suited figure in their garden, looking at them through the bay window. At the same time the TV set suffered from severe electrical interference.

Tall faceless figures, "giants" and spacemen, were also seen at Herbrandston and many other places. One figure was seen at the Haven Fort Hotel on the way to Little Haven. There were examples of radio and TV interference connected with other sightings. And there were a number of descriptions of strange flying craft overhead, on the ground, and approaching Stack Rocks and in the bay. Some swore that they saw great doors opening in the rock, with the UFOs passing inside, and with small figures clambering all over the rock itself.

Over the space of a few months in the Spring of 1977 these sightings reached almost epidemic proportions, with frequent reports in the local press. The sightings had ceased by the Summer of 1977, and we still do not know whether the St Bride's Bay area (and maybe RAF Brawdy in particular) was really targetted by aliens. The strange space-suited individuals and their vehicles certainly caused chaos for a while, but they appear to have been entirely harmless, and that must make the locals sleep a little easier in their beds.

Date : 1977   Sources : Pugh & Holiday, Paget, Brooks p.80

7.18 Tenby and the Beggar's Curse

During the seventeenth century Tenby was a fine town with its prosperity based upon rich fishing grounds and fine trading vessels. But according to an old tradition the decline of the town's fortunes can be dated to one terrible event involving a deaf and dumb beggar.

A few years before this event, some pirates anchored their vessel in Caldey Roads and sent a spy ashore to investigate the town's wealth and study its defences. The spy was captured and examined by the town's Mayor, but during his trial he pretended to be deaf and dumb. Nonetheless, he was found guilty of spying and he was executed on the gallows on Gallowtree Hill.

So it was that when an old deaf and dumb beggar entered the town the people refused to believe he was genuine. The Mayor could prove no crime, but in any case he offered a reward to anyone who would flog the old man and teach him a lesson. A citizen called Leekie Porridge accepted the offer. He siezed the terrified old man and carried him off to the Norton end of the town. The poor fellow fell upon his knees and pleaded through his gesticulations for mercy. But Leekie Porridge showed no mercy, and the sentence was carried out in front of the assembled townspeople.

The beggar was so badly injured that he lay still for a long while, having been left for dead. But at last he managed to climb up a track called Slippery Back at the side of the cemetery, and reached a point above the chapel. There he fell on his knees, and stretching his hands out over the town he cursed the place and its people in silence and in agony. Next day he left the town, never to return.

At once, the fish left the fishing-grounds and Tenby began a slow but inexorable decline. The merchants and their trading-vessels fell upon hard times, and the hardship continued until the last man who had sanctioned the cruel outrage against the beggar had died. As for Leekie Porridge, it is said that he and his children were unable to grow beards for four generations. Vengeance was brought down upon the Mayor also, for his only child was struck dumb and his wife died as a result of the beggar's curse.

Date : c 1650 ?   *Source : Bielski p.74*

Opposite:
In any case he offered a reward to anyone who would flog the old man and teach him a lesson . . .

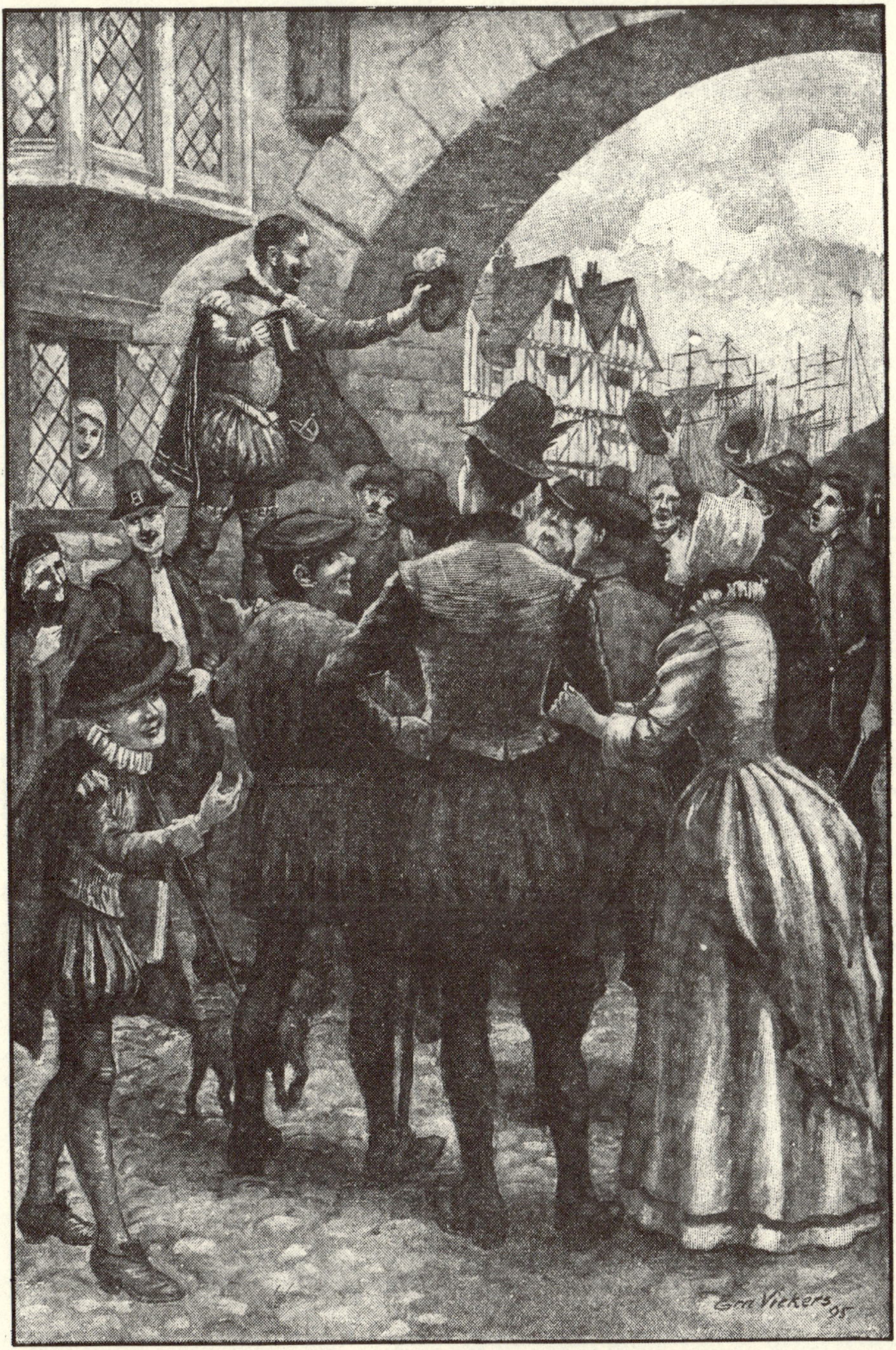
Vickers 95

7.19 Premonition at the Rising Sun

It was blazing June in the year 1922. There had been a good spell of hot dry weather, and the hay was ready to be cut at Dolrannog Uchaf, a farm on the flank of Mynydd Carningli, not far from Newport. While the weather held Mr William Ladd, the farmer, arranged with his neighbours that they should all help out on Wednesday; and a communal day of convivial toil was in prospect, just like many other such days on the other farms around Cilgwyn.

Mr Ladd and his wife knew that there was going to be a great demand for provisions, for it was the tradition that the farmer should feed the workers during the day and provide abundant quantities of ale into the bargain. Haymaking was thirsty work, especially in hot weather. So on Tuesday afternoon Mr Ladd set off on his pony towards Newport, intending to do his shopping in the town before returning fully laden with provisions. The journey proceeded calmly enough, with the pony trotting along quietly even though bothered by the heat and by the swarms of early summer flies. As pony and rider drew parallel with the "Rising Sun", a little inn about half a mile from Newport, the pony suddenly stopped and refused to go one step further. Mr Ladd dug his heels in, and used his whip, and cursed and swore at the animal, but it still refused to budge. At last he had to dismount, and it was only after a great deal of cajoling that the animal consented to be led past the inn. Then the farmer re-mounted, and the rest of the trip to Newport went off as normal.

In the town, Mr Ladd related this strange incident to various shopkeepers, and all were mystified by it. Later in the afternoon, when the farmer was on his way home, he rode up the hill towards the "Rising Sun" and exactly the same thing happened in exactly the same place. Mr Ladd, now furious with his pony, had to dismount and drag it past the inn; and indeed he was so disturbed by the incident that he felt not in the least inclined to pop in for a jar or two. When he reached home and had unloaded his provisions, he told his wife what had happened, and she too was mystified since the pony was normally very placid and obedient.

Next day, when all the haymakers turned up at Dolrannog for the day's work, it was noticed that one man was missing. It so happened that he lived in the cottage next to the "Rising Sun". One or two people began to feel concerned as to his whereabouts, and decided to go down to his cottage to check. On arriving there, they discovered that he had committed suicide during the night.

Date: c 1922   *Source: word of mouth*

7.20 The End of Trefloyne and Scotsborough

There were once two fine mansion houses not far from Tenby. One, named Trefloyne, was the seat of the Bowen family; and the other, named Scotsborough, was the seat of the ap Rice family. According to legend, both families were involved in the wrecking business, placing false lights to guide trading vessels to their doom. For a while the families profited greatly from this activity, but around the year 1700 their dastardly deeds caught up with them. At that time there was only one son of the ap Rice family and one daughter of the family of Trefloyne. It so happened that both were coming home from abroad on the same vessel. As it approached Tenby after dark it was led astray by the false lights and wrecked on South Sands. Both young people were drowned.

After this it was as if a curse was laid on the two great houses. Scotsborough gradually declined. By the early years of the nineteenth century it was largely ruinous and the west front was converted to house a number of poor people. But in 1824 smallpox broke out and the inhabitants fled in terror, never to return. The building soon collapsed. Trefloyne went the same way, so that when the naturalist Gosse visited the area around 1850 the mansion was but an ivy-covered ruin.

Date : c 1850   Sources : Bielski p.79, Fenton p.7

7.21 Phantom Funeral at Milford

Around the year 1810 the grandfather of Mr John Pavin Phillips of Milford Haven shared a strange experience with seven or eight members of his family. They lived not far from the new parish church of St Katherine's, and their house in Pill was separated from the churchyard by two meadows. One fine summer evening the family were sitting outside their front door enjoying the setting sun when their attention was attracted by a funeral procession approaching the churchyard. They all saw a crowd of mourners following the coffin, which was borne on men's shoulders. The procession passed along the pathway towards the church, and it was met by the parson, whom the watchers all recognised. The parson then led the procession into the church for the funeral service. In due course the parson and the mourners emerged from the church, and proceeded to the corner of the churchyard, where in the normal way the burial was completed.

Mr Phillips and his family were astonished by what they had observed, for they had not been aware that any funeral should have taken place in the church on that day and at such a strange time. Someone was sent over to the church to enquire who it was that had been buried. Soon he returned with the information that there had been no funeral service, and that nobody had been buried. The family were greatly puzzled by this and it was concluded that they had observed a "fetch funeral". Sure enough a few days later one of the neighbours died quite suddenly. His funeral was held in St Katherine's church, and the burial took place in exactly the spot in the churchyard where the ghostly burial had occurred.

Date : c 1810   Source : Underwood p.121

7.22 The Ghost of Princess Nest

One day in 1975, a family was enjoying a picnic lunch in the car-park across the millpond from Carew Castle. It was a fine summer's day - not at all the sort of day for ghost watching. However, suddenly the mother noticed the white figure of a woman moving about among the castle ruins. The members of her family then all saw the same figure, now in one place, then disappearing behind a wall, and then seen again somewhere else. After watching the figure for a few minutes, one or two members of the family crossed over to the castle to see whether they could find the shadowy figure and watch her from close at hand. But on reaching the castle and searching among its crumbling walls, they found nothing and heard nothing. The figure had quite disappeared.

Many other people have also seen the White Lady at Carew, and the "ghost watcher" Peter Underwood has another virtually identical record of a sighting by another family, again with the first sight obtained by the lady of the family. On other occasions the appirition has appeared at the high windows, where there are no internal floors to support the weight of normal human beings.

It is widely thought in the Carew area that the White Lady of Carew Castle is the ghost of Princess Nest. She was the daughter of Rhys ap Tedwdwr, one of the most powerful princes of South Wales. She was renowned in the Middle Ages as the "Helen of Wales", for she had enough adventures in and out of bed to provide the raw material for many a romantic novel. She married in the year 1100, at a very tender age, the same Gerald of Windsor who figures in another story in this volume. She lived in Pembroke Castle, but her real home was Carew which was passed over to Gerald as part of the marriage dowry. Nest's beauty was renowned throughout the whole of Wales, and many men desired her. On one occasion she was visited by her second cousin, Owain ap Cadwgan. He was immediately overcome with love, or lust, and determined to abduct her. Accordingly, when she was staying with her husband at the castle of Cenarth Bychan, Owain and a dozen companions dug a tunnel beneath the castle gateway, set fire to some of the outbuildings in order to create a diversion, and surprised the sleeping inmates of the castle. It appears that Nest was not averse to the idea of being carried off in Owain's arms, and indeed she encouraged her husband to make his escape while she remained behind with her children. She and the rest of her family were duly carried off into the depths of Ceredigion by the hot blooded Owain.

The outrage reached the ears of the King and the Bishop, and a confederacy of Welsh princes was organised in order to rescue Nest and her children and to punish Cadwgan and his son by confiscating their territory. Father and son could not resist the forces ranged against them, and in due course they fled to Ireland, leaving Nest to be restored to the arms of her husband Gerald.

Later on the beautiful Nest enjoyed further adventures, becoming the wife or mistress of Stephen the Constable of Cardigan, and also a mistress of King Henry I. But it is said that her true love was Owain, and that her ghost wanders amidst the walls of Carew Castle awaiting his return.

Date : c 1110 ?   Source : Underwood, p.47, Laws p.108

7.23 The Castle Hotel Ghost

The Castle Hotel in Little Haven is reputed to be haunted, and a number of visitors to the hotel have had strange experiences there over the past thirty years or so.

In September 1972, Mrs Aileen Ash and her husband were staying at the hotel. One night they went to bed at about 10.30 pm, falling asleep almost immediately. Sometime later Mrs Ash awoke with a start, having a distinct impression that she heard footsteps approaching the bedroom. She thought at first that someone must be going on upstairs, passing their room in the process. But then she realised that they were already at the top of the stairs, and that there were no higher rooms in the hotel. She became petrified with fear as the handle on the bedroom door turned, and the door slowly opened. In recalling the incident she recalls that she could not move a muscle, not even to nudge her husband and wake him, much less to switch on the bedside lamp. Someone, or something, walked across the room towards the bed, and Aileen distinctly heard the floor-boards creaking as the footsteps came closer. As she lay listening intently and with her eyes wide open, the presence seemed to turn round and go back towards the door, for the floor-boards creaked again. Then she heard the door closing as the visitor left the room. Eventually Aileen managed to relax after this strange episode and went back to sleep.

In the morning she told her husband what had happened, and they were both mystified when they examined the floor and discovered that it did not creak when someone walked across it. They talked to the landlord, John Gibson, about their ghostly visitor, and he told them that the floor of their bedroom used to creak very badly but that it had been re-laid a few years previously in order to eliminate this particular problem. He also told Mr and Mrs Ash that occurencies such as that described by Aileen were not uncommon in that particular room. They all decided that the ghostly visitor was quite harmless, and the couple continued to sleep in the room for several more nights without experiencing anything unusual.

Date : 1972 *Source : Underwood p.83*

7.24 Lucy Walter of Roch Castle

Lucy Walter was born in Roch Castle (or in the village of Rosemarket) around the year 1630. She spent part of her childhood here and part of it in London, not in the happiest of circumstances since her mother and father spent most of their time in dispute over financial matters and over the custody of their children. When Lucy was seventeen her father obtained custody of the children by a ruling of the House of Lords, and it appeared that she might settle down at Roch Castle.

But these were turbulent times, and the Civil War brought trouble to many families around West Wales. Lucy's father William Walter originally garrisoned the castle for the king, and indeed the Royalist connection was a strong one since his wife was related to the Royalist commander the Earl of Carbery. In 1644 the castle was taken by the Parliamentarians, but it was re-taken by the king's men four months later. According to legend, Oliver Cromwell himself was present during the castle siege, and young Lucy (who was 14 at the time) hurled a javelin at him from a high window, missing him by inches. She then managed to escape from the castle under cover of darkness.

Before the onset of the Second Civil War (1648) it was apparent that more trouble was in the air, and William sent young Lucy off to Holland in the care of an aunt. What happened after that is difficult to unravel, but it appears that the young lady captivated Col Robert Sydney and became his mistress. After that she spent some time in The Hague, and met Charles Stuart who was later to become King Charles II. On 9th April 1649 she gave birth to Charles' son, who was named James and who later became Duke of Monmouth. According to rumour, Lucy and Charles were actually married, but this was always hotly denied by the King in later years. In any event they spent some time together with their new baby in July and August of 1649 in Paris and St Germain. In 1650 Charles left for Scotland, but Lucy was not particularly faithful to her Prince and promptly became involved with the future Earl of Arlington, bearing him a daughter.

In 1656 she returned to London, but it was inconvenient to have her in free circulation and she was arrested and clapped into the Tower of London. Parliament in its wisdom decided to deport Charles' "lady of pleasure" and she was shipped back to the Netherlands. Charles was given custody of his son. Lucy found her way to Paris, and by the time young James was nine years old his mother was dead, having lived the last two years of her life in wretched conditions, quite abandoned by those in whose company she had delighted only a few years before.

As a teenager Lucy must have been very beautiful, and contemporaries described her as healthy and brazen. But she lived a sad and tortured life, with few moments of happiness. Some of these moments must have been during her childhood in and around Roch, and it is said that the castle is still haunted by a slightly-built young lady in a white dress who appears at windows and floats through locked doors from one room to the next. Running footsteps are heard now and then in the middle of the night, and many guests in the castle (which is now used for self-catering holidays) have been awoken by this sad presence.

Date: 1647   Source: Miles, p 104; Brooks, p 67

PEMBROKESHIRE FOLK TALES

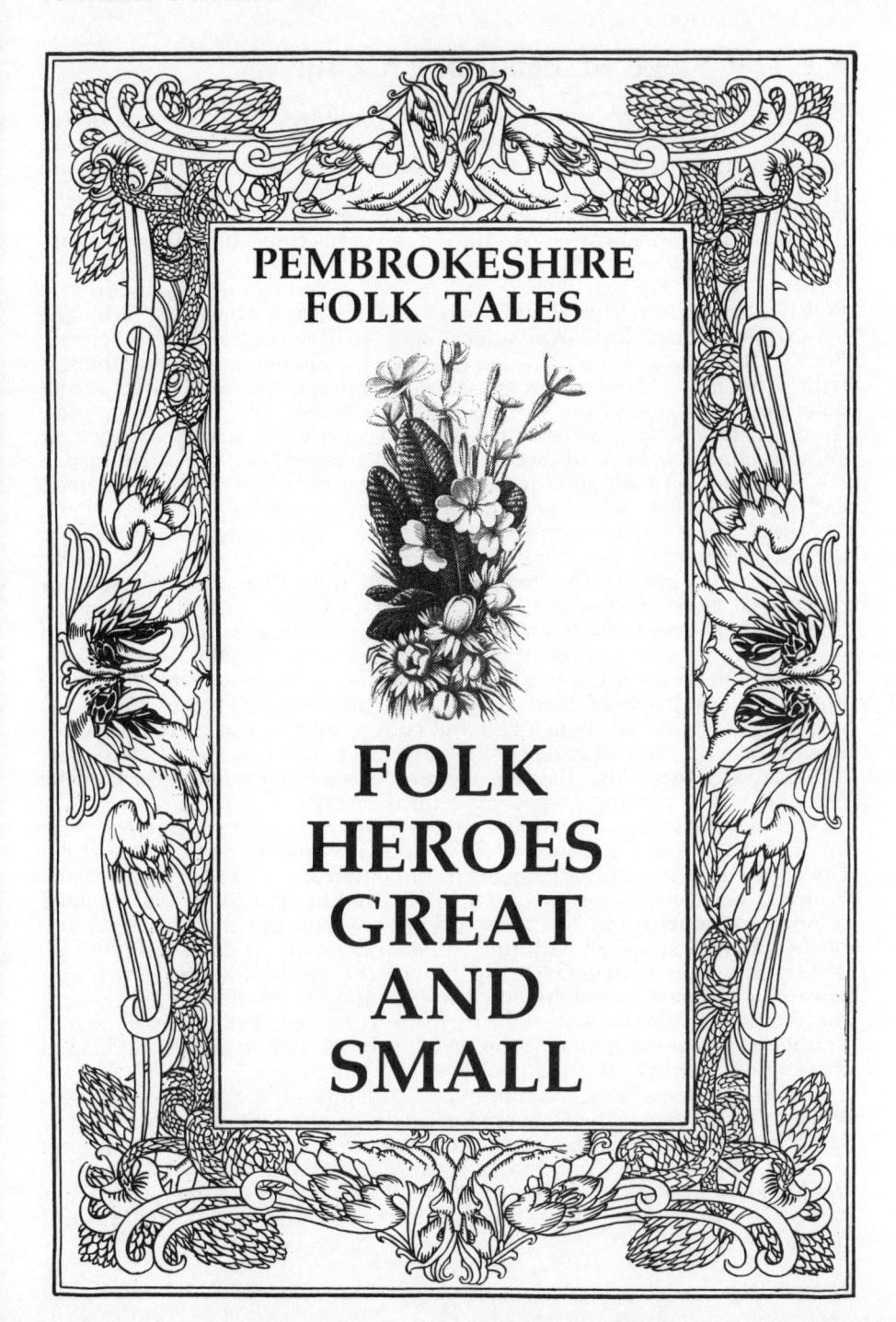

FOLK HEROES GREAT AND SMALL

8.1 The Siege of Pembroke Castle

The first Norman fortress at Pembroke was built by Arnulf of Montgomery in 1091, using stakes and turf as his raw materials. It was not a very powerful structure, but at the time the Normans had their hands full with the unruly Welsh, and there was not a lot of time available for castle-building projects. Arnulf moved on to further conquests in 1093, leaving the castle and a small garrison in the charge of his constable and lieutenant, Gerald of Windsor.

In the following year Gerald had to face a formidable assault from a Welsh army under Uchtryd ab Edwin and Hywel ap Gronw, and it looked for a while that the Norman invaders might be driven out of Pembrokeshire. But Gerald was a resourceful leader who would not give up without a fight. The first attack was repulsed, and since the defenders appeared determined to resist, the Welsh leaders decided to starve them out. Accordingly a siege was established; the Welsh army simply sat in their encampment just beyond arrow range, and waited for the surrender.

Things did not look good for Gerald and his men, especially since food and water supplies were very low. Matters were not helped when fifteen of Gerald's best knights decided to desert, and were caught attempting to flee in a boat across the Pembroke River under cover of darkness. Gerald was naturally furious. He stripped them of their titles and immediately transferred their estates to fifteen of their own men-at-arms, whom he dubbed there and then as knights. The siege continued until Gerald and his men were on the verge of collapse from starvation. But Gerald knew that the besieging army was also getting restless, and he decided to risk all in a desperate game of bluff. There were only four live pigs left in the castle, but Gerald had them killed and cut up, and he hurled the pieces of fresh meat over the battlements at the attackers. This had the desired effect of convincing the Welsh that the fortress was well supplied, and that the Normans were possibly expecting reinforcements.

Next day Gerald dreamed up an even more ingenious stratagem. He knew that Wilfred, the Bishop of St David's, was staying at that time at the Palace of Lamphey, only two miles from Pembroke. So he wrote a letter to Wilfred, which he then signed and sealed, stating that there was no need of reinforcements from Arnulf for at least another four months, since the castle was well supplied with provisions and water. At dead of night one of Gerald's men managed to slip out of the castle and made his way towards Lamphey, "accidentally" dropping the letter while passing one of the Welsh encampments. Gerald correctly surmised that the letter would find its way into the hands of the Welsh princes, who read it and decided there and then to call off their siege.

The Welsh army struck camp and set off to look for new adventures, leaving Gerald and his beleaguered garrison greatly relieved. According to some historians, the lifting of the Pembroke Castle siege was the turning point of the Norman Conquest in West Wales. From that point onwards the invaders inexorably tightened their grip on South Pembrokeshire and carved out for themselves the territory later to be known as Little England Beyond Wales.

Date : 1094 *Sources : Giraldus p.148, Roderick p.19*

8.2 The Pontyglasier Boulder

Once upon a time a smallholder called Jack lived on a little farm near Pontyglasier, beneath the great sweeping moorland on the north side of the Presely Hills. He had a few rough acres of land, and in one of his small fields a very inconvenient boulder projected through the ground surface, causing damage to his plough every time he cultivated the land. One evening he and his friends took it into their heads to remove the boulder.

So next morning they all set to work with a will, and with pickaxes and shovels dug deeper and deeper around the edges of the boulder. It turned out to be an extremely large boulder. By nightfall they had still not managed to move it, but there was a deep trench all around it, surrounded by piles of mud and stones thrown up by the diggers. Next morning, when Jack and his neighbours returned to the task they found that it had rained heavily, and the trench was full of water, with the tip of the boulder standing up like a little island in the middle. So they had a conference and decided to dig a long trench down to the corner of the field in order to drain the water away. This took all of the second day.

On the third day the trench was dry, and the warriors returned to do battle with the boulder. Deeper and deeper they went, and at last they reached the bottom of the boulder. But try as they might, they could not pull it out of the hole. So they decided they would need some stout timbers to lever the boulder up bit by bit, and some stones to wedge beneath it, thereby lifting it higher and higher until it could be rolled away from the hole. Several small trees had to be cut down from the nearby wood to provide the levers, and a section of the stone wall around the edge of the field had to be demolished to provide the stones. And so the third day passed.

On the fourth day the friends began to lever up the boulder, packing smaller stones beneath it and heaving and straining on their stout timbers. Higher and higher it came, until at last, with a great roar of triumph from the labourers, the mighty boulder rolled away from the hole and settled on the surface of the field. This deserved a celebration, so the men spent the rest of the day recovering from their exertions with the aid of a few pints of home brew.

Next day, being the fifth day, Jack and his friends did not feel too good, having worked too hard and drunk too much. But on returning to the fray they realised that the boulder was now more of an obstacle than it had been before, since it was sitting on the surface of the field and was too heavy to move any further. So they called in another neighbour, who happened to be handy with dynamite, and having assessed the situation he reported that it would be no trouble at all to shatter the boulder into small pieces. So everything was made ready, and after a few pints of home brew the appointed time came. There was a mighty explosion which echoed all around the neighbourhood. And when the smoke cleared the men discovered that the boulder was still intact, having settled into a huge crater that had miraculously appeared beneath it. Only a small part of the boulder was above the ground surface, and as the friends watched the sides of the crater caved in, enveloping the rest of the boulder with mud and stones.

At that point Jack and his friends gave up in disgust, and returned for a few pints of home brew. Jack never touched the field again, and that is why, to this day, close to the hamlet of Pontyglasier there is a little field with a large pit full of boulders, surrounded by a sort of embankment, with a long trench running downslope. Nearby there is a gap in the woodland, and a section of the old stone wall which marked the field boundary is missing. There are nettles and brambles and bull rushes where once fine crops of hay were cut. And close to the large pit the top of a boulder can be seen, just projecting through the ground surface.

Date : c 1982   Source : word of mouth

(Opposite) *For a while confusion reigned around the mansion......*

8.3 Tough Times in the Wild West

There have been some very strange squires in Pembrokeshire history, but none more eccentric than John Laugharne, Squire of Llanrheithan between 1726 and 1751. He was the last squire to inhabit the old mansion, located in the wild west midway between Abercastle and Solva. His adult life was spent in a futile attempt to keep his estate intact and to fight off the financial claims of a host of people including his three awful sisters and their three awful husbands. Most of the quarrelling over money and property was done through the courts, but there was a great deal of picturesque skulduggery as well.

Squire Laugharne enjoyed the good life, and in the 1730s he was renowned in North Pembrokeshire for his hospitality and generosity. He was the last of the Pembrokeshire gentry to keep a jester, known as "Ffwl Llanrheithan", whose antics endeared him to his master but proved to be a sore trial to all guests. But as time went on the estate fell upon hard times and he was unable to maintain his three sisters in the manner to which they would like to have been accustomed. One court case followed another, and as the world closed in on him the embattled squire determined to defend himself by establishing a small private army of retainers.

Now things began to get exciting. In 1740 the under-sherriff arrived at Llanrheithan with a posse of stout fellows to seize goods to the value of £200, which sum the squire had refused to repay to a neighbour in spite of a court order from the Quarter Sessions. For a while confusion reigned around the mansion. The posse seized 30 cattle, but the squire summoned up his forces and in a pitched battle recovered the beasts and sent the sherriff and his posse limping back to Haverfordwest, sorely battered and bleeding. Writs and court orders were now issued with alarming frequency, as is the way when vultures appreciate that their prey is not in the best of financial health. But serving the writs on Squire Laugharne was easier said than done, for his faithful bodyguards were all around, and patrolled the grounds of the mansion by night and day. Llanrheithan became an impregnable fortress; nobody got in without passing the guards, and the squire never went out.

Local attorneys offered substantial rewards to anyone who would serve a writ on John Laugharne, but even the toughest of men refused, being in terror of the squire's private army. The only writ to be successfully served on the squire was delivered by an intelligent and very beautiful young lady called Elinor David, who was employed by an attorney called John Stokes.

Elinor arrived at Llanrheithan one fine day in April 1743, trotting along sedately on horseback and wearing her prettiest dress. She tied up her horse outside the main gate and walked up the drive, nodding sweetly to the fierce armed men who confronted her and innocently asking to see Mr Laugharne. The squire never could resist a pretty lady, and invited her into the parlour for a drink. Elinor then handed him an envelope which she said contained a letter, which was not urgent and could be read later at his leisure. He stuck the envelope in his pocket and went to the back of the house to fetch the sweet girl a glass of ale. When he returned, with his mind full of romantic thoughts, she was gone. Furiously he tore open the envelope and discovered that it contained a writ for £210 due to Attorney John Stokes. By this time Elinor was beyond the main gate, galloping away and in mortal fear for her life. The squire mounted his best steed and rushed off after her, but Elinor and the attorney had placed fresh horses at intervals along the road to Roch, and by using these she just managed to keep ahead of the squire until she reached her own home.

This adventure proved only that it was one thing to issue a writ against the Squire of Llanrheithan but another thing to enforce it. More writs, summonses and court orders followed, all totally disregarded by the squire. At last he was declared an outlaw, but having been informed by his spies that a body of men was being dispatched to arrest him and sequester his estates, John Laugharne escaped by night and went into hiding for two years. There is no record of where he was during this time, but legend has it that he was somehow mixed up in the Jacobite rising of 1745. Eventually he returned by stealth to Llanrheithan in 1746. But news of his return leaked out, and around Christmas 1746 he was captured "by a stratagem" and thrown into the County Gaol at Haverfordwest.

The squire remained in gaol for over 18 months, during which time the legal mill-stones ground inexorably, reducing his estate and his family fortune to the point where there was hardly anything left. In July 1748 he attempted to escape while being escorted from the gaol to the courthouse, but was thwarted by a man with a bludgeon. At last he was released while the final details for the disposal of his assets were worked out. But he was a man of some spirit, and he soon recruited his private army again and managed to hang onto most of the property that remained in and around the mansion. One day when the vicar arrived during the harvest to collect his corn tithes he was seen off by Laugharne and his merry men, who opened fire with assorted primitive fire-arms. The man of God responded by capturing the squire in September 1749 and giving him such a severe beating that he almost died. The muscular vicar was successfully prosecuted for assault, but in November the poor squire was beaten up again by the Peters family of Llanrheithan Mill. Then, in December, the High Sherriff and an armed posse stormed the mansion house and took possession of all the contents.

In the following year the squire managed to regain some of his possessions, and again he recruited his armed guards and fortified the mansion. But now there was little left to defend, and the eccentric Mr Laugharne was arrested again in 1751 and thrown for the second time into Haverfordwest gaol. While he was there the bulk of the estate was sold off by the administrators, and the Squire eventually discovered that all he had left in the world was the sum of £72.14s.5d. realised from the sale of various assets. On his release from gaol he went off to England, to return two years later with a wife and baby daughter. He moved back into his beloved mansion, which he had been allowed to retain, but he was soon struck down with a fatal illness, and he died in December 1755. He was buried in the little churchyard above the mansion.

So ended the sad but lively tale of the Squire of Llanrheithan. The old mansion fell into disrepair, and was demolished in the early years of the eighteenth century. Now it is lost without trace, but it is said that the ghost of John Laugharne can still be seen in the twilight, near the footbridge over the stream close to his beloved home.

Date : 1755   Source : Francis Jones, Pembs Historian 3, p.53

8.4 Tall Tale from Goodwick

Shemi Wâd (James Wade) of Goodwick, who died in 1887, was a renowned story teller or *cyfarwydd*. His tales were tall rather than short. This is one of them, recounted by Shemi himself and then told and retold a thousand times by others in the inns of Fishguard and Goodwick.

Shemi had gone fishing down on the Parrog, the broad expanse of marsh and sand-dunes between the two towns. His strong fishing-line was in the water, with a dozen hooks all baited, waiting for the fish to bite. It was a hot afternoon and Shemi felt sleepy, so he retreated up the bank, first tying the line around his waist and then nodding off to sleep on the warm flank of a sand-dune. While he slept the tide went out, and since no fish had been biting the baits were all exposed on the mud-flats. The seagulls liked the look of them and swallowed the lot - hook, line and sinker. Then something disturbed the gulls and the whole flock took off, carrying Shemi with them, still fast asleep. They flew all the way across St George's Channel, landing at last in Dublin's Phoenix Park.

In due course Shemi woke up to find himself, in the failing light, in strange surroundings. He realised he was in Ireland, and feeling somewhat concerned about his safety in this strange land he looked for somewhere to hide. Around the edges of the Park he saw a gallery of large guns. Here was the answer, thought Shemi - and he slipped into the barrel of a cannon and went off to sleep. He did not know that a salute was fired from the guns every morning; and so it was that the still sleeping Shemi was shot out of the gun barrel, to fly straight back across St George's Channel. As luck would have it, he landed on the soft green grass of Pencw, right above his home.

Afterwards Shemi swore blind that every detail of the story was true, and all his listeners swore blind that they believed him.....

Date : c 1880   *Source : D.W. James, Pembs Mag 48*

8.5 The Vision of Rosebush

Back in the mid-1800s the village of Rosebush, not far from Maenclochog, was nothing more than a cluster of four primitive hovels and a little slate quarry. The place was, so far as we know, not even blessed with a name. But then the owner of the quarries, Edward Cropper, had a vision of great developments, and he determined to transform this bleak windswept spot into a sort of Arcadia.

In his dream Edward Cropper saw the slate quarries enlarged and flourishing, served by a busy railway line. He saw a thriving community served by a shop and a hotel, with ornamental gardens where people could walk and enjoy the long summer evenings. He saw the hamlet developed as a spa resort, attracting thousands of visitors to the Presely Hills where they could find "health and repose".

So Cropper heroically set about the task of transforming the dream into reality, supported by his family. He invested greatly in the slate quarries and replaced the four poor cottages with a "quarryman's row" of 26 terraced dwellings which became known as "The Street". A windmill was erected to pump water into the quarries, and a water supply from a pool in one of the quarry pits was piped to the growing settlement. Water from the pool was also used for driving machinery in the quarry dressing-shed, and for a series of splendid ornamental fountains which were established in the pleasure gardens. A magnificent corrugated iron hotel was built for the guests who were expected, and finally plans were made for the completion of a railway line from Clynderwen via Maenclochog to Rosebush.

The railway was the key to the success of the whole enterprise, and on 19th September 1876 the line was opened. There were free rides along the route, and all the visiting dignitaries were entertained to a grand luncheon in a marquee erected at Maenclochog, with two brass bands providing music in between the lengthy speeches. In its first full year of operation the line was busy with loads of slate being shipped out to markets in South Wales and further afield, while about 24,000 passengers were conveyed on the line.

Unfortunately Edward Cropper did not live to see his dream come true, for he died in 1877. But his family was determined to see the project through, and entrusted the management of the Rosebush enterprise to his stepson John Macaulay. The young man was enthusiastically supported by Colonel John Owen, second son of Sir John Owen of Orielton, who had married Cropper's widow. Both Macaulay and Owen believed that Rosebush was an ideal place for a mountain resort, since it was now so accessible by rail and was in any case in such a beautiful environment. Plans were made to extend the railway line through to Fishguard via Puncheston and Letterston, and work on the ornamental gardens and other facilities pressed ahead.

But the good times did not last. The railway line to Clynderwen was bumpy and noisy, and passenger numbers dropped off in spite of an aggressive advertising campaign involving colourful posters and special ticket offers. The quality of slate in the quarry began to decline, and at the same time top-class slate from the huge quarries of North Wales began to flood the market. The "spa" waters of Rosebush proved to have no medicinal properties whatsoever, and progress on the railway line to

Puncheston was painfully slow. When the traveller Thornhill Timmins visited Rosebush in 1894 the windmill was derelict, the station was "defunct", and it was rumoured that in seventeen years the line had progressed barely four miles. Shortly after the turn of the century the quarries closed down, and although the line to Fishguard was now complete its success was short-lived, for the main line from Clarbeston Road to Fishguard through Treffgarne Gorge opened in 1906.

From this point on Rosebush began its sad decline, with the railway lifted in the First World War, relaid, damaged during practice bombing runs in the Second World War, and finally closed for good in 1949. Now Rosebush is a place of memories, but those who visit it can still share in Edward Cropper's heroic vision. The Precelly Hotel is still there, looking as if it has been miraculously transported from Port Stanley in the Falkland Islands; the great slate quarries still dominate the bleak moorlands; the quarrymen's row is still intact and still lived in; traces of the old railway track and railway station are still to be found; and what is left of the ornamental gardens is still worth exploring. And what of the picturesque name? Probably the name "Rosebush" was dreamt up as a piece of marketing hype, designed to entice those thousands of Victorian holiday-makers who, sadly, decided to go elsewhere.

Date : c 1890   *Sources : Miles p.40, Morris p.20*

8.6 The Fools of Strumble Head

Once upon a time there were some foolish fellows who lived at Llanwnwr, near Strumble Head. They bought a round cheese at Fishguard Fair. Just as they reached home, the fool who was carrying the cheese dropped it, and it rolled downhill along the lane leading to the sea. They chased after it, not too fast, in case they should overtake it. One of the fools jumped over the hedge and ran on the other side, as one does when one is driving cattle. Soon the cheese came to the cliff edge and rolled straight over, crashing down into the sea far below. The fools agreed that they could get at it by hanging over the edge of the cliff, each one taking hold of the ankles of the one above. When all was ready, with all three dangling in space, the top fool said "Let me get a better grip. I must spit on my hands." And down they all went after the cheese, never to be seen again. Strangely enough, the heroes of this story are immortalized on the map, for the bay closest to Llanwnwr is still called Pwll Ffyliaid (Bay of Fools).

Date : c 1750 ?   *Source : T.G. Jones p.232*

8.7 The Curse at Plas Glynamel

Richard Fenton inherited the Manorowen estate from his uncle Samuel in 1796. He was a good landlord, and he was noted for his benevolence in and around Fishguard.

Soon after his accession to the estate Richard Fenton began to build a fine residence for himself in the Gwaun Valley not far from the village of Cwm and adjacent to an old cottage called Carn y Garth. He decided to call the new house Plas Glynamel and to hold a consecration ceremony at the laying of the foundation stone, and many of the local gentry and common people assembled for the occasion. Just as the vicar concluded the ceremony with a blessing, an old woman called Anne Eynon rushed out of the crowd, accompanied by her small daughter, and began bitterly to denounce the Fenton family. In an uncontrolled fury she screamed a famous curse, as follows: "I curse you. I curse your children. I curse your home. From the day you enter it, misfortune will follow you; your sons shall fall into dissention, and sickness upon yourself. The one you choose shall not succeed you! And with the third of your name who comes into possession, the place shall pass from your family. And God told me last night that my girl should live until she sees all my curses fall upon you and yours."

Naturally enough, this greatly embarrassed the assembled company, and pleasure and enjoyment gave way to doubt and uncertainty. But Richard Fenton quietly took the woman aside and asked why she was so upset. She replied that she had looked after Samuel Fenton in his old age, and that in return for her devotion the old man had promised her a meadow and the cottage of Carn y Garth. But he had failed to keep his promise, and no mention was made of her in his will.

The new squire became deeply depressed by the curse, but he did what he could to restore the faith of the old lady by granting her nominal ownership of the land at Plas Glynamel and paying her an annual rental of £30. He provided her with a comfortable house and garden, where she spent the rest of her days comfortable and well fed. Plas Glynamel was completed, to become one of the most beautiful buildings in the Fishguard area, with grounds planted with exotic shrubs and trees. In a further gesture of goodwill to old Mrs Eynon, the squire gave a job to her daughter as a nursemaid to his two younger children.

But neither the old lady nor her daughter ever lost their bitterness, and the daughter frequently reminded the Fenton children about the curse. John, the eldest son, grew up to lead a dissipated life within the social circle of the Prince Regent in London, and caused great disruption within the family. He had a number of furious disputes with his father, and when the old man died suddenly in 1821 it was discovered that John had been left out of the will. Richard's chosen heir to the estate was his second son Charles, who was a parson. But Charles unexpectedly passed the estate back to his elder brother, who wasted its resources and continued his exotic lifestyle until there was little left. On John's death the estate was inherited by a third Fenton, who promptly sold it, thereby fulfilling the prophecy of old Anne Eynon. Shortly after this, her daughter died, having seen everything come to pass.........

Date : c 1800   Source : Ferrar Fenton, Miles p.67

8.8 How the Wiston Estate was Won

The basilisk was a fierce beast (thankfully now extinct) only a foot or two long, but with a black and yellow skin, poisonous breath, and eyes both in the front and back of its head. There was a particularly terrible one living in its den a hide on a hillside near Wiston, and this one could kill human beings simply by looking at them. On the other hand, if anyone could look at the basilisk without first being seen, the beast would die.

About 700 years ago there was a dispute between various claimants to the Wiston estate, and it was agreed that the estate should go to the person who could kill the basilisk by looking at it while still remaining invisible. After several claimants had tried unsuccessfully to outwit the basilisk, signing their own death warrants in the process, one bright young man hit upon an idea. He climbed into a barrel and rolled down the hillside past the beast's lair. Peeping out through the bung-hole, he shouted "Ha! Bold basilisk, I can see you but you can't see me!" In this way the basilisk was killed, and the young man became the owner of the Wiston estate.

Date : c 1290 *Source : Roberts p.23*

8.9 The Flying Trousers of Twm Waunbwll

Thomas Phillips of Glandwr, near Crymych, was a famous local character in the early years of this century. In Welsh he was known as "Twm Waunbwll" after the name of his farm to the east of the little hamlet. In addition to the tall stories told by him to others, there are many tales still in local circulation about his eccentricities. When he died in December 1914 there was great local sadness, for he was held in affection by the whole farming community of the Crymych area and the lower Teifi Valley.

Twm used to catch the local train (traditionally known as the "Cardi Bach") to Cardigan market every Saturday. He used to travel with a great sack into which he would dump all his weekly shopping -- meat, tea, sugar, fish, nails, candles, bread and everything else. One day, on his walk to the station at Llanglydwen to catch the train, he sat by the roadside for a little rest. Later, as he got to the station, he started to feel distinctly uncomfortable, and concluded that he must have been sitting on an anthill. Once he was aboard the train the itching became intolerable, and Twm decided that there was nothing for it but to take his trousers off and give them a good shake. With the train now going along at a fine pace, Twm opened the carriage window, leaned out and shook his trousers energetically to get rid of the ants. However, they filled with air and were torn from his grip. Twm and his fellow passengers watched with fascination as the trousers sailed off into the sky, receding rapidly into the distance as the train chugged on serenely towards Cardigan.

Undeterred, Twm continued into the town and did his shopping as usual, attired in hat, tweed waistcoat and jacket, black boots, and violently striped Welsh woollen long johns..........

Date: c 1905 *Source: James Williams, p 76*

8.10 Seithennin and the Drowning of Cantre'r Gwaelod

The north coast of Pembrokeshire once marked the southern margin of Cantre'r Gwaelod (Bottom Hundred) at a time when sea-level was lower than it is today. Much of the land now submerged beneath the murky waters of Cardigan Bay was fertile and beautiful, with 16 wealthy fortified towns and a busy and contented population. The land was protected from the sea by a great embankment and sluices, which were opened at low tide in order to let the river water out, and then closed again as the tide rose. It was a great honour to be Keeper of the Embankment, and at the time of this story the appointment was held by one Seithennin, the son of the King of Dyfed. But although he was of royal blood, he was later remembered as "one of the three immortal drunkards of Britain".

One day, reputedly in 520 AD, the Lord of Cantre'r Gwaelod, one Gwyddno Garanhir, was holding a great banquet for his nobles. As the revelry reached ite height, the guests were entertained by a harpist, who suddenly warned them that doom was at hand, and cried out to them that they should flee. King Gwyddno, however, held up his hand. "Do not worry, my friends," he said. "There is nothing to fear, for the gates and embankment are in the good hands of Seithennin." But then the assembled guests noticed that Seithennin was sprawled in the corner of the banqueting hall, utterly oblivious to the peril which confronted them. As warned by the harpist, he had forgotten to close the sluice gates as the tide rose.

Panic broke out among the guests. They shouted and screamed as they scrambled for the doors of the hall. But it was too late. As the wind howled and the waves lashed against the embankment, the sea flooded through the open gates and rose remorselessly, flooding the whole of the Lowland Hundred and causing the death of most of the population by drowning. Some people, including King Gwyddno and the harpist, escaped to North Wales. Next morning, as the king lay on the beach, looking out over the endless expanse of grey water across Cardigan Bay, he could find no words to express his horror. Instead, he uttered a mighty sigh which echoed along the shore and across the waves. Cantre'r Gwaelod was never reclaimed from the sea.

Those who live along the present coastline will tell you that out to sea, when the water is clear and the weather calm, you can still see the ruined buildings on the sea floor. And if you listen carefully, you can still hear the church bells sounding faintly beneath the dark waters.....

Date : 520 AD   *Sources : G. Jones, p.197, Roberts p.6, Parry-Jones p.119*

8.11 Black Barty of Little Newcastle

Bartholomew Roberts was born in Little Newcastle in 1682, the son of poor farming folk who brought him up to be honest, God-fearing and hardworking. When he was ten years old he went to sea; and so he embarked on a spectacular maritime career which was to make him the most famous pirate of all time. He was dead before he reached the age of 40, but he managed to cram a considerable amount of living into his short time on this earth.

Barty became third mate in a slaving vessel plying between Africa and America, but in 1719 his ship was attacked by pirates led by a fellow Welshman, Hywel Davies. Barty and Hywel took a liking to each other, and when Hywel offered the young man a job as first mate on his pirate ship, the **King James,** he leaped at the opportunity. Piracy offered better prospects for a poor uneducated Welshman than did the merchant navy, and Barty opted deliberately for "a merry life and a short one".

The new pirate was a good companion, a skilled navigator and a natural leader of men, and when Hywel Davies was killed only six weeks later in a skirmish with another vessel, Barty was elected captain in his place. From then on Barty ruled his men with a rod of iron, allowing no gambling, no quarrelling, no alcohol, no women on board, no smoking below decks, and no piracy on Sundays. He was a strict teetotaller all his life, preferring to drink China tea; but he loved music, always having a wind band on board; and he loved flashy clothes, preferring to dress in flamboyant scarlet from head to toe when going about his work. But in spite of his eccentricities he was an excellent captain, greatly admired by his men. He even provided them with a sort of pension scheme, and those who were injured in action were often retired onto dry land with cash enough to set themselves up in style.

During the next two years, Black Barty took over 400 ships, with a total value in gold of over £51 million. His seamanship and his bravado were greatly admired, even though the merchants and navies of Spain, Portugal, Great Britain and other seafaring nations treated him as Public Enemy Number One. Most of his triumphs were achieved without a fight, for Barty was a master in the art of sea warfare, always using his small and manoeverable Welsh collier the **Royal Revenge** to great effect. He was also

His seamanship and bravado were greatly admired . . .

renowned for his dislike of unnecessary violence. The women passengers of captured vessels were invariably safe in his hands, and their captains were invariably invited to tea and musical entertainment with Barty while their holds were relieved of their treasure chests. His most famous capture was the Portuguese **Segrada Familia,** a huge warship which contained the entire treasure of the King of Portugal - worth £21 million.

Barty then moved north and became the terror of the New England coast, causing the English government to construct forty fortresses in a vain attempt to protect the colony from the sea. Barty and his men razed many of the fortresses to the ground, and burned or sank many of the vessels that supplied the colony.

He also terrorized the coasts of Africa and the West Indies. Governors pleaded with him to desist, and he was even offered a free pardon by King George I. But when he invited the King and Parliament to be "damned with their Act of Grace", something had to be done. At long last, a task force of two frigates under Commander Ogle was sent to hunt down this obstinate and irreverent Welsh pirate who was the scourge of the high seas.

In 1722 Ogle shadowed Barty along the coast of Africa, becoming more confident of success since the pirate had now exchanged his little Welsh collier for a larger and more cumbersome French vessel called the **Victoire.** The vessel was loaded down with loot, and Barty now had so much treasure that he needed two other smaller ships to carry it about. His little fleet was beginning to become unmanageable, and maybe he was beginning to consider himself pistol-proof after two invincible years at the helm. But for whatever reason, Barty was out-manoeuvred by Ogle when the critical confrontation came. The naval commander first tempted one of Barty's smaller ships into a gun battle; and having disposed of that one he moved in with his superior fire-power and engaged Black Barty himself. There was a fierce battle with hand-to-hand fighting, and Barty was killed by a sniper's bullet, the marksman having been attracted by the pirate captain's magnificent scarlet outfit.

So died Barty Roberts; so died a legend; and so ended the great age of piracy. Ogle returned a hero, and since nobody asked about the whereabouts of Barty's treasure, he mysteriously became a very rich man. But Barty is still remembered as one of Pembrokeshire's famous sons, as the man who invented the skull and crossbones, and as the man who gave the pirate flag the name "Jolly Roger". For it was Barty himself, with his swagger, his wit and good humour, and his scarlet clothes, who was referred to by his French enemies as "le joli rouge".

Date : 1722   Sources : Worsley p.48, Brinton & Worsley p.166, Miles p.82

8.12 Trouble for an Amorous Bard

One of the Welsh heroes of the Late Middle Ages was Dafydd ap Gwilym, a bard or wandering scholar who wrote some of the most beautiful and lyrical poetry in the Welsh language. He was born in the Teifi Valley around 1340 and died around 1400, having lived most of his life in Dyfed. He travelled widely throughout Wales, welcomed in all the great houses and patronised by the Welsh princes and their families. He made his living like most bards in writing and performing his poetry, but unlike most of the older bards he wrote hardly at all about politics and war, and concentrated instead on poetry about love and the beauties of nature. His poetry had a lightness of touch that was quite exceptional, and as his reputation grew he became known as a "chief poet".

Perhaps Dafydd's greatest attribute was his ability to tell good stories in his poetry, with great humour, normally at his own expense. This story comes from one of Dafydd's poems, probably written when he was a young man around the year 1365; and for decades afterwards it must have been a popular folk-tale, repeated over and over again amid storms of laughter in hostelries all over Wales.

One day Dafydd came to a fine city. We do not know which city it was, but we can presume that it was Haverfordwest, not too far from his home area, growing rapidly at the time and already anglicised to the extent that Welsh travellers were treated with some suspicion. Dafydd was feeling in a good mood, so he took lodgings in "a rather high class inn" for his young servant and himself. He ordered some good quality wine, and spotted a slim and pretty girl who was "as fair as the rising sun" among the guests. Not being a man to waste time, Dafydd immediately invited the bashful girl to his table for a roast meal and a few mugs of his wine. She agreed, and one thing led to another. Dafydd became quite infatuated with the girl; he spoke two magic words to her which had the desired effect, and he promised that he would come to her bed when everybody else in the inn was asleep.

At last all was quiet, and when he was convinced that the girl and himself were the only ones still awake Dafydd embarked upon what he later called "his dreadful journey". It was a pitch black night, and there was not a single lighted candle anywhere in the inn. First of all Dafydd fell over something, making a great noise in the process. He got up, groped his way across the floor, and then fell over a stool which the landlord had carelessly left in an inconvenient place. This created more noise, but in spite of the fact that some people must by now have been awake our hero was inflamed with passion and continued towards his destination. In rising, Dafydd banged his head against the edge of the table, knocking a basin and a copper cooking pot to the floor. Temporarily stunned, he leaned against the table, inadvertently pushing aside one of the trestles so that the whole table collapsed. There was an almighty racket as pots, pans, dishes, cutlery and beer mugs all crashed to the floor, waking up every person in the inn and causing the innkeeper's dogs to start barking as if the end of the world was at hand.

By now three Englishmen named Hickin, Jenkin and Jack, who lay "in a smelly bed next to the high walls", were wide awake, and quite convinced that Dafydd was up to no good. "There's a sneaky Welshman prowling about here," spluttered Jenkin, "and he's up to no good. He'll rob us if he can. He's a thief. Be on your guard!" And they grabbed their packs and stared into the darkness as Dafydd tried to hide. Now pandemonium reigned. The landlord roused everybody in the inn, lighting candles to assist in the search for the unknown criminal. Dafydd hid himself away silently in a dark corner while the search parties ranged high and low, and prayed "passionately from the heart". At last, by the grace of Jesus or through sheer good luck, he found the opportunity to return to the sanctuary of his own bed, and dived beneath the covers while the commotion died down.

For the rest of the night he lay wide awake, battered and bruised, and (according to the old poem) thanking the saints for their intervention and begging God for forgiveness. No doubt the bright young girl with the black hair lay wide awake too, thinking her own very private thoughts......

Date: c. 1365   *Source: Lofmark p 92*

8.13 Shemi's Wager

It was a thirsty night in Goodwick, and the inns were doing a roaring trade. There was talk, and laughter, and dim lights, with ale spilling onto the sawdust floors with increasing frequency as the night wore on. Shemi Wâd was in the Rose and Crown, greatly enjoying himself. The talk turned to the drinking abilities of those present at the bar, and there was a bit of an argument. Somebody challenged Shemi that he couldn't drink eight pints of ale on the trot. Shemi was not a man to pass up a challenge, and so a wager was made. Two gold sovereigns were deposited with the innkeeper, and a time was fixed for the contest the next evening. The betting was fast and furious, as the Rose and Crown regulars assessed Shemi's drinking abilities and put down their money on the outcome of the contest.

Next evening a great crowd assembled in the Rose and Crown at the appointed time. The pint pots were made ready, and more money changed hands as the men waited for Shemi to turn up for the fray. But Shemi did not appear. At last some of the regulars started to mock Shemi, claiming that he had turned yellow and had ducked out of the contest. Laughter began to echo around the bar.

But much later in the evening, with the contest time long since past, Shemi appeared at the door. "Come on, Shemi!" shouted one. "Shame on you, Shemi!" shouted another. "Have you given in then? Is eight pints too many?" The bar became quiet as the men all waited for Shemi's reply.

"No, No, boys bach," replied Shemi, after a theatrical pause. "Eight pints is no problem. I've just been in the Hope and Anchor next door, getting in a good bit of practice. **Now** I'm ready. Where are those eight pint pots, then?"

Date: c. 1875   *Source: David James, Pembs Mag 48*